To: Dave

Best [signature]

Go Pack Go!!

To: Dave & Phyllis

THE TRUE SPIRIT OF COMPETITION

BRADY POPPINGA

Copyright © 2014 Brady Poppinga.

All rights reserved. No part of this book may be reproduced, stored, or transmitted by any means—whether auditory, graphic, mechanical, or electronic—without written permission of both publisher and author, except in the case of brief excerpts used in critical articles and reviews. Unauthorized reproduction of any part of this work is illegal and is punishable by law.

ISBN: 978-1-4834-1251-1 (sc)
ISBN: 978-1-4834-1252-8 (e)

Library of Congress Control Number: 2014916983

Because of the dynamic nature of the Internet, any web addresses or links contained in this book may have changed since publication and may no longer be valid. The views expressed in this work are solely those of the author and do not necessarily reflect the views of the publisher, and the publisher hereby disclaims any responsibility for them.

Any people depicted in stock imagery provided by Thinkstock are models, and such images are being used for illustrative purposes only. Certain stock imagery © Thinkstock.

FOREWORD

By Bronco Mendenhall (head coach,
BYU Cougars 2005-present)

My players know me to be a purpose-, vision-, and principles-driven coach who is tough and hard-nosed and expects the highest level of commitment and dedication. I value hard work over talent and contribution over entitlement and believe respect is earned, not guaranteed.

Brady Poppinga was a junior when I arrived at BYU as the defensive coordinator (2003). Our first interaction was as he passed me in the hall of the football offices and said, "What's up, buddy?"

"Buddy?" I asked. "We have a long way to go before you call me that."

I just kept walking and passed by him. Things did progress in a much more positive vein after expectations where clearly established and I could see Brady's intense desire to compete at a higher level.

An example of that was on September 4, 2004. BYU was scheduled to open the season at home against Notre Dame. In the week leading up to the game, I tried to help each defensive player visualize in his mind that we would not allow the Irish to run the ball against us. Not a single inch. My defensive staff and I designed our defensive team and position group meetings and practices such that during every film clip reviewed, every lift, every drill run, every formation called and scrimmaged play, we emphasized the point that the Irish were not going to run the ball on us. As a leader on defense, Brady captured that vision himself and ensured he and his teammates were prepared to compete at that extraordinarily high level.

That game Notre Dame ran the ball twenty-one times for eleven total yards, and BYU won, 20–17. Brady led our team in tackles, tackles for loss, sacks, quarterback hurries, and about every other defensive category that night. All of our defensive players exuded confidence and executed at the highest level due to their visualizing what was asked of them and why. They prepared and executed in practice at the same high level that they did during the game.

Upon being named head coach of the BYU football program in December 2004, I felt the whole football team needed to unite around the same vision and purpose of why we play football at Brigham Young University. We weren't all on the same page in terms of who we represented, what was expected of us, or having one culture in which we competed. At the time we had one culture for the defense and another for the offense. We represented a university that was unique from any other, and we needed to figure out what our distinctness and differentiation needed to be as we competed.

In order to compete at the highest level, we needed first to have a clear, compelling mission, vision, and set of objectives. To support that unified mission, we needed to identify a few principles that could drive a shared culture to get BYU football back to a national prominence it had lost. In order to create this distinctive culture in which to compete, we chose three powerful principles: accountability, discipline, and effort. I believe the worst mistake

I can make at BYU is to not ask enough of our athletes—in all aspects of their lives.

Lasting happiness comes from what I believe are the four most important things in life—faith, family, knowledge, and friends. These building blocks are critical to our happiness both short and long term. They are essential parts of life that will ultimately influence who we are and what we stand for.

I feel it is an honor and a blessing to coach football where I have a wonderful game to teach great principles and design experiences where young men have an opportunity to grow and develop. I believe it is a great sport for providing opportunities to learn teamwork, strategy, discipline, leadership, best practices, and you get out of it what you put into it. I believe football develops life skills and knowledge that can be applied at home and in their careers, their communities, and their faith.

Brady was one of those outstanding young men who was a joy and privilege to teach and coach. It has been a wonderful experience to follow his career and talk to him about what he calls the "true spirit of competition." I love how he relates this to the whole person, spiritually, mentally, morally, and physically. I believe that through the stories and experiences of Brady's life, athletes and nonathletes alike will benefit from learning how the principles, practices, and knowledge of competing from a deeper place have a major impact on higher levels of performance.

THE TRUE SPIRIT OF COMPETITION

1

DREAM IT TO BE IT

As I walked out of the tunnel into the sold-out, standing-room-only stadium, the buzz of excitement from the seventy thousand fans in attendance was palpable in the air. The green grass was perfectly manicured, like carpet. The fans standing on either side of the tunnel gave me fist pumps as they wished me good luck; today was the championship game! Winning the championship in our own stadium and in front of our own fans was an unseen driving force. The smell of freshly cut grass mixed with the aroma of buttered popcorn that wafted up from the snack bars under the stadium. The fans were enjoying barbequed brats, hamburgers, and hotdogs outside of the stadium as the tailgating festivities were finishing up in time for the game to start. I was dressed in my game uniform, a white jersey with matching white pants. The uniform had navy blue pinstripes with my last name on the back of my jersey. I was wearing number ninety-eight. This was the moment I had waited for, to live and experience.

The game was of typical championship caliber, with both teams worthy of taking the title. It was like a heavyweight fight, with each team exchanging blows to the very end. With under two minutes to go in the fourth quarter, we had the ball and were down seventeen to twenty-one. We needed four points to tie the game, so we had to score a touchdown for the win. This final drive would determine if we won or lost the championship. The only thing was, we had to start our drive around the ten-yard line. With ninety yards to go to win the game, everything was on the line. We drove the ball consistently to the opponent's thirty-yard line and now faced a fourth and long following three incomplete passes.

This play was the game. The announcer picked up the action. "Poppinga drops back to pass. The game is on the line, folks. Ohhh! What a play by Poppinga! He threw a dart to—who is it? Number ninety-eight, Poppinga, on the sideline, down to the ten-yard line for a first down! And as soon as Poppinga caught the pass and turned upfield, the free safety flew in there like a heat-seeking missile and chopped Poppinga's legs out from under him, causing Poppinga to flip head over heels on his back. Oh, what a clutch play! And what a big hit! Both these teams want this game bad, folks.

"The clock is winding down, under ten seconds, they'd better hurry up! The ball was barely snapped right as the clock struck zero. Poppinga drops back to pass. He throws a jump ball to a receiver in the corner of the end zone. The receiver is being covered by two defenders. It looks like any one of the three could have come up with the ball. Oh my! The ref is signaling touchdown. Yep, Poppinga, number ninety-eight, looks like he caught the pass! They won the championship! Another spectacular play made by Poppinga!"

When I caught the ball for the winning touchdown, the cheer of the crowd was as deafening as a jet engine. My whole team ran

THE TRUE SPIRIT OF COMPETITION

from the sidelines and dog piled on top of me. We had just won the championship. In the midst of all the pandemonium and the roar of the crowd, I could faintly hear a voice piercing through all of the noise. It was my mother's voice saying, "Brady, it's time for dinner." A little confused, I listened harder. My mom again called to me, but this time it was louder. "Brady, it's time for dinner!"

After finally understanding that my mom was calling me up from the basement for dinner, I put my football down, took off my plastic play football helmet, and walked upstairs to join my family for dinner. This was a daily ritual of mine. Every day after school, from the ages of six to twelve, I would come home and pretend play football down in my basement by myself. I was playing out a dream I eventually wanted to live: to play football on a big stage. I wanted to make big, game-changing plays in those games.

I dreamed of first playing for Brigham Young University, then after that in the NFL. After the movie *Rudy* came out, my parents told me that in some ways, I was very similar to Rudy. I was similar in the sense that I had my mind already made up at the young age of ten that I was going to don the Y on my helmet as a member of the BYU football team. Just as Rudy had dreamed of playing for Notre Dame, I had posters of BYU football players and pennants of the team hanging all over the walls of my bedroom. My parents would take my siblings and me to BYU football games in Provo, Utah, quite often. Every time I witnessed a live BYU game, I could see myself down on the field, flying around making plays. This continued to validate the fact that someday I was going to be a Cougar.

When I would pretend play football, I played all of the positions. I was the quarterback, the running back, the wide receiver, and the defensive players. I would play this pretend football in an area next to our TV room, which had enough space so I could run up and down the room and mimic playing a football game. Whenever I got tackled, I would run directly into our old, beat-up orange couch that my parents placed to the side of the room. I would run full speed into the armrest, which would hit me right below my hips, and I would flip head over heels onto my back on the soft couch cushions. I really enjoyed the experience of running as fast as I could into the couch and flipping over the armrest. As I threw the ball to myself and maneuvered past pretend defenders on my way to making a touchdown, I would talk like the announcer. Whenever I scored, I would make that white noise with my throat that sounded like the crowd going crazy and cheering me on in my play; I was a dreamer.

I pretended play football so much that it became ingrained in my subconscious. There was a time when I had just finished playing my pretend football game right before going to bed. I remember hugging my dad, saying goodnight, and then heading off to bed. The next morning, one of my brothers was chuckling, as he often did to tease me, as I entered into the kitchen for breakfast. I asked him, "Why are you laughing at me? What did I do?"

He began to tell me that after I had been in bed for ten to fifteen minutes, I had gotten up in my sleep and was running up and down the living room, pretending

Brady at the age of 2.

THE TRUE SPIRIT OF COMPETITION

I was making the winning touchdown in a game. I didn't believe him, but my dad, who was standing right next to my brother, confirmed that I indeed had run up and down that same living room area where I would go after school, pretending that I was scoring the game's winning touchdown. He said I was high stepping like Deion Sanders did whenever he would score a touchdown. Apparently after I scored, I again walked over to my dad to say goodnight. Then I went to bed again. I didn't remember one thing about this, but I was playing football in my sleep. I loved football so much that at times my mom would find me fast asleep with a football under my arm. I really loved the game!

My love of football started when my dad first brought home old pads from the rec center he ran in Evanston, Wyoming. I was about four years of age, and I remember him pulling them out of the back of his car. My elder brother, Casey, and I would be so excited that our dad had brought us football pads that we immediately put them on and went into the backyard. Up to that point, my brother and I had not received any formal instruction on how to play the game. We had only watched how the players played football on television, so we copied what they did. Our interpretation was running into each other as fast and as hard as we could. From that point forward, there was something about running myself as hard as I could into my brother that I really enjoyed. I also may have liked the game of football because I am a physical person, and I could run into somebody as hard as I could, knock him down, and not get into trouble for it. I was passionate about playing the game of football, and this is where my love for football began.

From that day forward, I watched football on TV. Whenever I would watch a game, it would motivate me to play myself. I would call up friends in the neighborhood and attempt to organize a football game at the nearest park. If no one was available, I would play by myself. That is where the pretend play began.

I was born as raised in Evanston, Wyoming, a very cold part of the world, where summers were short and springtime was often interrupted by heavy snowstorms. I began to play basketball and other sports that could be played indoors in addition to football. The thing I liked about basketball was that it was a sport that could be played regardless of weather conditions. I could always go to the rec center and find other boys my age playing pick-up basketball games, and that was important for young boys like me who needed to stay active. Although I spent much of my time participating in other sports, football was always my favorite. I enjoyed the physicality of the game. Unlike in basketball, I could knock someone to the ground and no one would call a foul on me. I liked that.

When I turned twelve, my parents signed me up for my first official year of tackle football. My father, who was always teaching me and my siblings how to play sports, like how to shoot a basketball, or how to throw a baseball, in this case wanted to teach me how to properly tackle. It was early September, a few days before my first tackle football practice, my father took me out to where all of his coaching would take place—in our backyard. My father lined up across from me and told me to stand still while he

Brady at the age of 10 wearing his little league football pads and his favorite BYU jersey.

walked through the proper tackling technique. He proceeded to teach me that I should first, get low as I approached the ball carrier. Then, when I arrived, to about a step or two away from the ball carrier to run through him leading with my face, head-up, in the high chest area, right below the chin of the ball carrier. Lastly, as I engaged the ball carrier to wrap up as hard as I could with a big bear hug, while running my feet trying to push the ball carrier backwards. After going over the basics a few times, my father then grabbed a football and pretended to run the ball. He told me to tackle him as he had just taught me. With the zeal of a hyper Chihuahua, I ran forehead first right into what seemed like a wall of muscle into my father's high chest area, as I engaged my father and then wrapped up my arms and ran my feet just like he taught me. My father with a half grunt and laugh would say, "nice job, just like that".

When I was finally able to play in official tackle football games, I was able to put to practice the sound technique of tackling that my father had taught me. I played with an aggressiveness to where whenever I tackled somebody I was sticking my face mask right into their chests. It seemed as though every tackle I made, the referee would say, "Son, don't lead with your helmet or face mask, you are going to get hurt or hurt somebody else." These interactions with this referee were always so confusing, because I was executing to perfection my Dad's technique of how to tackle. I was not trying to tackle with my head down that could potentially expose myself and others to injury. So, I ignored the referee and kept tackling like my father taught me.

Parents on opposing teams started to take note of my aggressive and punishing style. On one occasion there was a pitch play to where the quarterback of the opposing team pitched the ball to the running back to attempt to run the ball outside of the formation. From my middle linebacker position,

I had a bead on the ball carrier to the point to where when the ball carrier turned upfield, I met him head-on. Just like I was taught in my backyard by my father, running full speed, I put my face mask right under the chin and on the high chest area of the ball carrier, I wrapped him up and ran my feet as I exploded through him. The ball carrier launched backwards on his back with his shoulders landing first. As the ref blew the whistle, he laid there with snot bubbles and tears as he began to cry. After getting up off the ball carrier, l was enveloped with adrenaline and endorphins as the enjoyment of such a picture perfect tackle was equivalent to eating my favorite dessert. I could hear many parents in attendance gasping as they witnessed such a violent hit. Still lying there, his father trying to teach his son to be tuff, yelled from the sidelines, "Get up son! Getting hit is part of the game of football". Not all parents felt that way. The following week my father received numerous letters from the parents of opposing team's players that stated that their son will not play as long as I am on the field. That experience only confirmed that football and its high impact style was something that was very natural and enjoyable for me to do.

Even though I felt destined to play football, I was still very committed to being a good basketball player. Throughout my youth, I would get major cabin fever and would have to go outdoors to play. During the winter months, everything was frozen. I had the great idea of shoveling four feet of snow off of our family's sports court to play some basketball. Every day I would shovel as much of the court as possible until it was finally clear of snow. Then I would hope and pray it would be sunny enough for a few days so the bottom layer of ice would melt away so I could play basketball on concrete. Trying to play basketball on a sheet of ice was very frustrating.

I remember a time when I had cleared the court and the bottom ice layer had melted away. It was the beginning of spring, and I was ready for winter to be over. I woke to the sunlight streaming in through the shades of my bedroom window, which was in the basement of my parents' home. I was excited about the prospects of what another sunny day would mean. I put on my shorts and basketball shoes and grabbed my basketball. As soon as I could get a better look at what kind of weather we were having, all I could see was white snow. It had just snowed another ten inches! All of my hard work of clearing the outdoor basketball court was in vain. I was upset, but I didn't quit clearing the sports court until the days of playing basketball would come to an end.

During my high school years, I could see my dream of being a college football player very clearly. I was only four years away from that happening. I knew it was going to take a lot of hard work and dedication to reach my goal. I knew exactly what I had to do to develop enough size, strength, and speed to be a football player capable of playing at the level I had always dreamed about. What I had to do was lift weights, and fortunately for me we had a coach by the name of Coach Smith who implemented a very organized and sound weight-training regimen. I had always seen my elder brother lifting weights when he was in high school. I knew as soon as I became a freshman that I was going to follow the example of my brother and work hard at lifting weights.

My first time lifting weights, Coach Smith wanted to do some baseline testing to see where my strength levels were at. He did a one-rep max test, meaning he wanted to see how much weight I could lift at one time. That would be an indicator of where my strength levels were. I bench pressed, one time, 135 pounds. I squatted 200 pounds, and I power cleaned 135 pounds. Coach Smith didn't have anything to say about how strong I was. He put a plan together for me and told me to come back as often as possible. When I started to look at other students' max strength levels, I noticed that mine were a lot lower than most of the guys and right on par with the girls. At that time I was as strong as a girl. That made me realize even more how much hard work I needed to dedicate to training and conditioning. I had a long way to go.

The distance of how far I had to go, was only confirmed to me during my first football practice in high school. At this time I was playing mostly running back on offense and linebacker on defense. During that practice, because of how underdeveloped my legs were, I began to feel pain in my quads forcing me to not run full-speed while doing running back drills. Coach Smith, being a hard-nosed running backs coach, urged me to run full-speed or to get out of the drill. I knew that if I didn't attempt to fight through the pain, my chances of being able to strengthen my legs would be very slim. So, I persevered through the pain and Coach Smith's urging of wanting me to step out of the drills. After practice, Coach Smith found me and sternly stated that if I didn't run as fast as I could during practice, that he would have me sit out. I took his counsel very seriously. Although it took some time to get my legs into football shape, again the gap between myself and the older players, who seemed to have no problems going full-speed during practices, only seemed that much wider. Following my Freshman year of football, even though I was moving in the right direction towards my goals, I was still a long ways away.

At the end of my freshman year, following a year of working my tail off under Coach Smith's direction in the weight room, I maxed out again. All of my max weights rose exponentially. My bench was now 225 pounds, I squatted 315 pounds, and I power cleaned a freshman record of 245 pounds. I saw the fruits of my hard work that confirmed to me, that even though I still had a ways to go, I was gaining ground on achieving my dreams.

THE TRUE SPIRIT OF COMPETITION

Because of hard work and consistency, and also having been blessed with good genetics, I continued to make the same jumps in strength that I saw my freshman year. Leading up to my sophomore year, I accompanied my elder brother, Casey, to the BYU football camp. Casey was being recruited by a lot of division one schools, and BYU was one of them. They wanted to take a closer look at him and invited him to come. My dad thought it would be a great idea for me to go with my brother and show the BYU coaches what I could do. When I practiced for the first time on their practice field, I was in football heaven. From the BYU practice field, there was a perfect view of the Y mount. It was a mountain that had a big Y on it. I remember thinking, *This is where I want to be, and I am going to get there.* Following the camp, to my surprise, the linebacker coach at the time, who was named Coach Schmidt, pulled me aside and said he was really impressed with how well I moved for my size. He said he wanted to see me again next year to see how much bigger, faster, and stronger I would get. I told him I would come back.

My sophomore (1995) year of football started off a lot better than my freshman year did. I was in tip top football shape. I was as big, strong and fast as any other player on our whole high school varsity team. What a difference a year makes! Since the varsity team only had a total of three guys who weighed over 200lbs, myself, my older brother and one other offensive linemen, the varsity coaches wanted to use me in a variety of ways. In one game I played offensive guard, offensive tackle, tight end, running back and on defense I played linebacker. Whenever I switched from a skilled offensive player to an offensive lineman I would have to run to the sideline and change my jersey from a forty number to a sixty number.

My best game of this year was the last one of the regular season. We were playing one of our rivals Green River, WYO in the final game of the season. They utilized a punishing rushing attack. That was exactly my cup of tea. Even though we lost that game, I ended up leading the team in tackles and to my surprise, won the media's choice for the defensive player of that game. After this game, I could see that I was really starting to make headway towards where I wanted to be.

In the latter part of my sophomore year I had a setback. During the basketball season I experienced a severe muscle tear in my hamstring. It was so severe that my movement skills really degenerated to the point to where I lost much of my speed and explosiveness. While doing conditioning drills during the spring, no matter how hard I tried to run my fastest, every step it felt like someone was stabbing my hamstring with a sword. The pain was so debilitating that I was being outrun by some of the slowest guys on the football team. Frustrated, because I feared that if I went to the BYU camp in that condition, my dream of playing football for them may not come to fruition. I limped off of the field and decided to do the most challenging thing to recover. That was rest. It took a good two years for that hamstring injury to fully heal, but fortunately for me less was more in this situation. Because after a few months of rest I felt almost back to my normal self. Just in time to for the BYU football camp.

When I went back to the BYU football camp, even though I was sore and I could still feel the aftermath of my hamstring injury, I put on a good display of my abilities. I was bigger, faster, and stronger than the previous year. Coach Schmidt came up to me and said, "Looking good, big fella." After hearing him say that, I felt that my day of putting on the BYU football uniform was a very good possibility in spite of having to deal with such a serious hamstring injury. Following that year's camp, he told me to once again come back the next year so he could check on me.

THE TRUE SPIRIT OF COMPETITION

Brady celebrating the 1997 Wyoming State championship with his teammates.

The following year going into my senior year, on the heels of a very solid junior year in football, was the time when colleges were aggressively recruiting. I went back to the BYU camp, anxious to prove I was ready to be a division one football player. After a couple of days of drills, Coach Schmidt pulled me aside and had me run a forty time that would measure my speed. After running a couple of forty-yard dashes, he pulled me aside and explained that BYU wanted to extend a full-ride football scholarship to me. Chills went down my spine. I thought back to those days when I had dreamed about playing for BYU and playing pretend football in the basement by myself. I thought of all of the time I had dedicated to lifting weights and working on my conditioning, and I realized I was now going to live that dream. My soul was filled with the euphoric adrenaline rush that comes with daring to chase and eventually realize your dreams.

My final year (1997) of football at the high school level was a special one. Not only had I received a scholarship offer from BYU, which fulfilled a lifelong dream. As a team all of our hard work paid off major dividends. Even though we started the year with a loss to Star Valley, who were on paper very inferior to us, we ended up ripping off nine straight wins to win a state championship and send off an excellent head coach, Coach Fackrel, into retirement as a champion. The improvement and progression that I experienced from a freshman in high school to the end of my senior year was dramatic.

What really drove me to put in the time, work, and sacrifice to achieve my dreams was my passion for competition. Growing up in a very competitive environment, I had the privilege of having an elder and a younger brother play vital roles in pushing me to higher echelons of performance that I could not have attained without them. But the number-one challenge I faced in my youth was reeling in my passion for competition—or better said, my passion to win.

2

WHEN THE PASSION TO WIN SPIRALS OUT OF CONTROL

It was a very frustrating one-on-one basketball game against my elder brother. It seemed as though no matter what I did, I could not get the ball over his long, outstretched arms and hands. He was blocking most of my shots, and he was making sure I knew he was doing a good job of it. Every time he blocked a shot, he would taunt me by saying, "Swat!" with a heckler's voice. Anger boiled inside of me because all I could think about was that I was destined for a surefire defeat at the hands of my elder brother. I knew very well that if he beat me, I would never hear the end of his badgering and bragging. I wanted the bragging rights. I needed to figure out some way of altering the eventual outcome so I could beat him.

As I schemed in my mind how I was going to beat him, I realized since I was a lot shorter than he was, I wasn't going to be able to block many of his shots. Since he was just as quick as I was, I wasn't going to be able to outmaneuver him neither. After exhausting all the ways I could possibly beat him in my mind, I realized my options were limited.

I got desperate. I wrapped my mind around the thought that it was better to defend my pride at all costs than to fall into the abysmal, dark hole of failure. I figured the only way to avoid the inevitable misery of defeat and failure was to play dirty. I needed to catch him in a place of vulnerability. When he went up to take his next shot, I pushed him in his exposed ribcage as hard as I could, hoping that would alter the inevitable outcome of defeat. Since my brother, being my opponent, in this moment formed the greatest threat to my glorious triumph, my defense mechanism targeted him, even if that meant physically injuring my own kin to come out victorious. He clearly wasn't too happy I did that. As soon as he recovered, he dropped the basketball and charged me like a bull. All of a sudden, a civilized game of basketball converted into a boxing match. Instead of finishing the game, we began to exchange blows.

During my upbringing, this type of hypercompetitiveness, of not ever wanting to concede a victory to my brothers, that was on display in a game of one-on-one basketball was all too common. Growing up as the middle brother of three was the perfect breeding ground for a highly competitive childhood. My elder brother, Casey, and my younger brother, Kelly, were very capable, athletic, smart, successful guys who had strong work ethics. Because of that, I had my work cut out for me to not only stay even with them but also to attempt to surpass them in all we directly or indirectly competed in.

I really looked up to Casey. Casey was the type of guy in high school who any father would want his daughter to eventually marry. He was tall, strong, athletic, and handsome. When he turned sixteen, he became an Eagle Scout. He was part of the

National Honor Society. He garnered all-American, all-state, and all-conference honors in football, track, and basketball by the time his high school career ended. He earned a full-ride football scholarship to the University of Wyoming (Following his mission experience he transferred to Utah State.). I had some big shoes to fill following in his footsteps.

From a young age, I studied in detail how well he performed in all of the sports we participated in our youth on up through high school to the professional ranks. I made mental notes of his accomplishments and accolades. I watched intently at how hard he played and how he interacted with his teammates and opponents. I did this for a two reasons. First, I looked up to Casey, and I wanted to follow in his footsteps. Fortunately for me, he was a great example to emulate. Second, I not only wanted to follow in his footsteps, but I also wanted to surpass him in everything. For example, in basketball I wanted to average more points and rebounds per game than he did during his high school career. In football I not only wanted to be all-state like he was, but I wanted to be a part of a state championship team. In my senior year in high school, I didn't want to be just all-state in football like Casey; I wanted to be all-state in both football and basketball.

Having an elder brother to look up to was a huge benefit for me. I was able to sit back and watch what Casey did. I was able to avoid some pitfalls that slowed him down. But because he didn't have many pitfalls, I spent most of my energy trying to live up to and exceed the high standards of success that he established.

In turn, there were great benefits of having a younger brother in similar ways. That is because my younger brother, Kelly, emulated me in much the same way I did my elder brother. I could always sense him watching very closely how I did things to see what mistakes he could avoid and what things he would try to mimic. I was always aware that he was going to try to surpass the standards

I set. For example, when I discovered that Kelly was going to be a discus thrower in track, it motivated me that much more to throw that disc as far as I possibly could so he wouldn't be able to break my school record. Because I could sense Kelly was trying to not only follow in my footsteps but surpass me, I was very motivated to set the bar high so he couldn't catch me. I wanted to keep ahead of him as much as I could.

I found myself smack dab in the middle of my elder brother, who I was always trying to catch up to, and my younger brother, who I was always striving to stay ahead of. I was in the middle of a competitive crucible of sorts, and I liked it.

Our relationships were defined by competition. One problem with this, was that I struggled in the heat of competition controlling my emotions. That meant in most competitive situations, I had a difficult time keeping in check my intense appetite for victory. So much so, I would go to the extremes of fistfights, wrestling matches, and arguments, all for the sake of winning. For example, my brothers and I would often compete head to head in almost any game. Whenever I would sense that I was on track for an eventual defeat, out came my natural inclination of wanting to defend my ego. I would go as far as cheating or bending the rules to try to avoid getting beat. This is where the discord began. Then, in an instant, we would go from arguing over the rules of the game to putting each other in headlocks.

Speaking from my perspective, this was my sabotage mechanism to avoid the darkness of defeat and somehow preserve my positive self-image. This was an all-too-common end to our head-to-head competitions. I was so competitive with my brothers that the thought of losing to either one of them was unbearable. Most of our head-to-head competitions would turn ugly by the time a winner could be determined. I do not remember ever finishing a one-on-one competition with my elder brother.

THE TRUE SPIRIT OF COMPETITION

Our parents must have felt like boxing referees because they were constantly breaking up our fights and sending us to our respective corners. They would encourage us to get along by reminding us that we were the only brothers we would have and that we should appreciate that. Those words went into one ear and out the other.

The fact that I had a strong passion and desire to win was not the root of the problem. The root of my trouble was I allowed this passion to become an obsession with winning. The obsession was triggered because I allowed the outcome of each respective competitive situation to form my self-worth. I was either the most successful person ever because I won or the worst failure to walk the face of the earth if I lost. Since I never wanted to accept defeat or deal with the feelings of defeat or failure, the fixation of avoiding them overtook me.

The saying, "Just win, baby" became my mantra. Whenever the outcome to a competition looked like I was destined for defeat, I morphed into a different person who had given up the guidance of my moral compass, leading me to attempt to bend or even break the rules of the game to come out victorious. For the sake of victory, it was worth it to me to treat my opponents harshly or mentally or even physically harm them. As long as I could walk away from any competition and preserve my successful self, I was okay with the collateral damage done along the way, even if it meant strained relationships with my friends or even my own brothers. Clearly this over obsession of winning wasn't good for my most important relationships—with my brothers. That was because I looked at my brothers as more of opponents than brothers. The problem was that from a very early age, I perceived my opponents as threats to my successful self. Unfortunately, this perception prevented me from developing amicable, brotherly relationships in my youth.

This primitive, wild-animal, survival-of-the-successful-self mentality that I competed with, that ignited my craze for winning brought me into negative places with undesirable consequences. However, whenever I took control of my competitive nature, that passion to win that I carried with me led me to very positive and lasting results. I would do almost anything to help my team win. There were times when I was in little league basketball that one of my friends who was on my team and I would go straight from school to the gym and practice shooting baskets. We would get out of school around three in the afternoon, and our games didn't start until seven in the evening. For four hours, we would practice honing our skills as shooters to give us the best chance to win.

On the flip side, I wasn't very sportsmanlike when my passion for winning escalated into an extreme obsessive compulsion with winning. One year in little league basketball, our team was facing a team with a kid on it who was a classmate of mine. For the entire week leading up to the game, I attempted to gain a mental edge by belittling his team's ability to beat us. I intended to make him think that no matter how hard they tried, they weren't going to win, so they might as well not even try that hard to save themselves the embarrassment of giving their best effort, only to come to find out it wasn't good enough. He obviously didn't agree with me about this. After a few days of build-up between this classmate and me, our respective teams faced each other on the basketball court. Like I had told him all week, we won. Instead of being a good sport, shaking his hand, and telling him, "Good game," condescendingly, I taunted him and gave him an "in your face" gesture, which he wasn't too happy about. He then proceeded to grab a basketball and threw it as hard as he could at my head. Luckily, the ball didn't hit me in the face, although I deserved it. When my father saw this, he was very upset with me, to say the least. Embarrassed, I left the gym. I knew I took things too far by rubbing our victory in his face.

THE TRUE SPIRIT OF COMPETITION

At that early stage in my life, I didn't recognize the real problem, but now I see how competing from a place of fear and insecurity fueled my dysfunctional behavior. My dysfunctional behavior really got out of hand later on in my high school years when I intentionally tried to physically hurt one of my teammates who I was practicing against. I remember this particular basketball practice during my senior year in high school like it was yesterday.

Worn out and exhausted from the rigors of the first part of practice, I slumped over and grabbed my shorts around my knees. I focused in on a sweat puddle as sweat was dripping off of my nose onto the dusty gym floor, creating a puddle. *Tweet!* The whistle blew to indicate we were going to begin our last session of practice. We were going to put all we had been working on in practice together and scrimmage. This meant that the other members of the varsity team and I were going to take on our "look squad." The look squad consisted of younger players made up of mostly juniors and sophomores. They would implement the strategies of our up-and-coming opponent to help us prepare.

These younger players were told to bother us and play an aggressive, in-our-face, pressing style of defense, up and down the court. Up and down the court they were out-hustling us, out-skilling us, and just flat-out beating us. I began to feel that if we couldn't beat our look squad, surely we wouldn't be able to defeat our upcoming opponents.

Again, this fear of having to deal with defeat and the feelings of failure surfaced. Then I lost control of my emotions as my passion to win was uncontrollably overtaken by an obsession to win. I became infuriated—not at myself because of my own ineptness but at the look squad. I irrationally blamed my feelings of insecurity, fear and self-doubt on them. Instead of investing my limited resources of energy in raising the level of my play to match or exceed theirs, I wrongly began to feel hostility toward them. Because of my feelings of anger and hostility toward the look squad, I wanted put fear in them. I mistakenly thought that if I physically inflicted pain on one of the junior varsity kids, I would intimidate them to the extent that they would relinquish their effort and let us win so we could regain hope that we could come out victorious in our upcoming game. My feelings of fear and self-doubt triggered this strong shift in my emotions.

When there was a loose ball rolling on the ground and up for grabs, I saw that as an opportunity to follow through with my delusional plan of action. As one of the members of the look squad took clear possession of the ball, I angrily wrapped my arms around him and body slammed him to the floor. Absolutely it was a direct infraction of the rules of the game of basketball. It was like something you would see in a WWE wrestling match—a picture-perfect soufflé.

Immediately the coach, who was very upset, pulled me aside and wanted to find out why I had lost my composure. In the moment, I really didn't see anything wrong with what I had done. I responded by saying, "I was mad because they were outplaying us to the point to where it was an embarrassment to me. I wanted to send them a message that if they continued to play as hard as they were, I was going to attempt to cool them off with my physical play." I felt that the varsity team's confidence would suffer knowing that we were struggling against our junior varsity team. How could we feel confident in ourselves to beat a varsity team if we were getting beat by a junior varsity team? That was how I rationalized my juvenile behavior.

The coach encouraged me to think about what I had just said and then asked if it was true that I wanted them to stop trying and let us win. "What challenge would that be?" he asked. I began to realize this was not what I truly wanted, and it probably would not develop my strength, skill, or even true self-confidence if those I was competing against did not even try to win. What really helped me understand my incorrect thinking was putting myself in their shoes and thinking of the times when I competed against guys who were bigger, stronger, and better than me, like competing against my elder brother for all of those years. I thrived in those situations as the underdog. I realized then that this was how those younger kids approached competing against us. As I empathized with the look squad my respect toward them grew. I respected the fact that they didn't back down, just like when I competed against my elder brother. I started to feel extremely guilty that I was trying to destroy their confidence. That didn't feel right.

The unfortunate thing about that experience was that it was not an isolated situation. It also was not the last time that I attempted to deliberately physically injure an opponent to not only try to gain a competitive advantage but also to compensate for my insecurities and to feel better about myself. There were other very similar situations that I justified as being the result of excessive passion of competitiveness on my part. When you start talking about excessive passion, you have most likely entered into the dark world of obsession. As I learned, the main difference between the two is when you're passionate about something or doing something, you grab hold of your passion to fuel the pursuits of your accomplishments. Obsession, on the other hand, is an overbearing force that grabs hold of you and takes you hostage.

Looking back, the more prudent choice would have been to make a greater effort to elevate my level of play and that of my teammates to exceed that of my opponent. That is how ability and true self-confidence are developed. Additionally, instead of trying to hurt someone to display my superiority, I should have gone out of my way to hug and thank them for pushing us to play our best in our upcoming games. Although that sounds like the more wise and productive approach to that kind of situation, when the opponent or outside force is viewed as a threat to your self-esteem, the thought of eliminating that threat is what becomes most important instead of the wiser approach of welcoming the forces as challenges to test your skill and ability. Obviously I lacked the capacity to bridle my passion for winning in the heat of competition. My extreme obsession with winning ignited because of a lack of true self-confidence that led to me seeing my opponents in a negative light. Something needed to change.

This is when the gears started to turn inside of me, and I began to see that the way I had viewed competition up to this point in my life was off base. Why couldn't I stay more poised in the heat of competition? Why did I feel so insecure? Why did I feel so threatened by my opponents? Why couldn't I compete against others and at the same time respect them? These were all questions I started to think about and wanted answers to.

3

"SPORTS IS LIFE WITH THE VOLUME TURNED UP" BARRY MANO

It was two in the morning. Darkness surrounded the lit-up basketball court located in downtown Evanston, Wyoming. The nearest stoplight was blinking yellow. The ball bouncing on concrete was the only sound heard at that hour of the morning. Most people were fast asleep but not me and my buddy Jeremy Jones. We had begun a one-on-one basketball game at ten o'clock the night before. The winner would be the first one to score eleven points, but he had to be ahead by at least two points to claim the victory. For the last four hours, neither one of us was able to build a lead of more than one point. We were very evenly matched. Jeremy and I were sweating profusely and tired as dogs. Neither one of us was going to concede to the other. We both were too competitive to say, "Hey, man, it's getting late. Let's go to bed." Finally, after a good four hours of aggressively competing, I was able to score two more points than Jeremy and won the game. This was one of many memories I thought of when I saw Jeremy Jones's parents sitting in the congregation at church.

I was sitting on the stand in church facing the congregation, getting ready to give my farewell missionary discourse. I would soon be leaving for a two-year LDS mission to Uruguay, South America. I saw most of the people who, second to my family, had taught me many key lessons in my nineteen years. I saw my friends I had competed with and against in sports through my youth and up through high school. I saw my sports coaches, scout leaders, school teachers, and Sunday school teachers. As I was sitting there reminiscing, all of the good times I had shared with these people came flooding back into my mind. I realized that most of these memories had to do with competing in sports. Up until this point, I had played sports almost every day as far back as I could remember. I suddenly realized that this next August was going to be the first August in almost ten years when I would not be playing football. I was missing my life of sports already. Now I would be entering a life of service and becoming a missionary, and everything I had grown to love in sports, throughout my childhood and up until now, would have to be put on hold for two full years. *This was going to be challenging!* I thought.

The first few months of my mission were eye-opening. My time was spent learning to be an effective missionary and learning the Spanish language in the Missionary Training Center (MTC) in Provo, Utah. Since I would be serving in Uruguay, I would be in the MTC for a good two to three months learning the language. It was late July, and football season was about to begin. This meant I would be in training right into the middle of football season. I made myself comfortable, as the MTC was my new home. One day as I was walking the grounds during a break, I found myself on the west side of the property with the sun glaring through the trees, illuminating what appeared to be bleachers. As I looked closer, it dawned on me that what I was seeing was the east end bleachers of Cougar Stadium. (Today it has since been renamed LaVell Edwards Stadium.) A feeling of awe overcame me, and I felt that I had beheld the most wonderful edifice known to man. The stadium I had always dreamed of playing in was literally a stone's throw away from where I was going to be staying for the next few months. I wondered if during the games I would be able to hear the crowd noise. I was going to find out!

As time passed, I learned the basics of the Spanish language, along with the Christian principles I would be sharing with the people of Uruguay. The main theme of those principles was founded on displaying deep respect to our fellowman. Clearly I wanted to live such principles, but in the heat of competition, adhering to them was always very challenging for me. At this time, though, my biggest concern was learning to be the best missionary possible. And this meant successfully communicating Christian principles in Spanish to the people of Uruguay.

One Saturday afternoon in late September, the leaves on the trees were starting to turn the beautiful colors of red, orange, and yellow, signaling the coming of fall. As I was walking from one building to another, enjoying the crispness in the fall air and the beautiful colors of autumn, I heard a big roar from a crowd coming from the west side of the grounds of the MTC. I immediately recognized what it was. It was the roar of a crowd at a BYU football game just down the street. When I heard this, my heart began to race, and my competitive juices started to boil inside of me. I instinctively wanted to run down the street onto the field, steal someone's football pads, and sneak onto the field just so that I could get a good shot on someone.

Constraining my emotions and myself, I walked into my next class session. I don't recall what was being taught during that session. All I could think about was that there was a game going on, and I could have been a part of it. To make things worse, one of my fellow missionaries, who was sitting next to the window, pointed out that I could get a glimpse inside of the stadium from our classroom. He said, "Hey, Elder Poppinga, you are not going to believe what I can see from our classroom. Come and take a look."

I got up out of my seat and walked over to the window. Sure enough, I could see right into the stadium. When I saw the fans sitting there watching the game, my longing intensified. I felt like I had in my youth as I would watch through the window as my brothers and the neighborhood kids played football and other sports in our backyard while I was inside doing my homework. I really felt left out!

This would come to be a defining moment in my life. I was standing on the threshold of stepping out of my very competitive sports life and walking into a world of being a missionary. Rather than being in the heat of competition in front of thousands of screaming fans and playing the physically intense game of football, I was in a classroom learning how I could bring a message of peace and love to the people of Uruguay. I was in the middle of two conflicting worlds. It was a distinct and clear point in my life where I was transitioning from the competitive world I had left behind and exchanging it for the world of being a full-time missionary who lived and preached the gospel of Jesus Christ.

Although I put on hold for two years my desire to compete as an athlete, I learned very quickly that even as a missionary, I would have to be competitive and fearless, just like I was facing three hundred–pound offensive lineman who wanted to engulf me. But instead of facing the likes of a three hundred–pound offensive lineman, I now had to face, in some ways, an even more daunting task: preaching in a foreign language to complete strangers while trying to adjust to a foreign culture.

THE TRUE SPIRIT OF COMPETITION

After arriving in Uruguay following a long plane ride, we pulled up in the taxi to a bland, single-story, brick, squared building with a blue tin door. I overheard my first companion, Elder David Wilson, who was my trainer, mention to me this was our home. We opened the blue tin door to the house, which screeched loudly. It smelled like mothballs mixed with a humid dustiness. To my immediate left, our *duena*, or landlord, was watching TV in her bedroom, as was her nightly ritual before going to bed. Like a worried parent, she stayed up extra late to ensure we arrived home safely and soundly. She also was excited to meet me, the new missionary. Elder Wilson greeted her, and she noticed we had safely arrived. She got out of bed to meet us and to welcome me to her house. Out of the TV-lit room appeared an older lady in her eighties with gray hair and a big, warm, toothless smile.

She said, "*Bienvenido.*"

I said, "Gracias."

She then sent us off to bed by saying, "*Buenas noches.*" She went off to bed. After that exchange, I thought being able to speak with the Uruguayan people would be no sweat.

Walking into our bedroom really struck my culture shock nerve. Unlike most homes I had lived in, there was no carpet. The tile floor around the house seemed grimy and dirty, like it hadn't been cleaned in months, although it was actually cleaned quite often. I sat on my bed, observing my new and foreign surroundings. Elder Wilson took off his shoes and socks and walked on the grimy tile floor barefoot, without any concern for how dirty it was. I thought, *No wonder why a lot of these missionary get the craziest sicknesses and diseases.* I took off my shoes and threw my socks, my other pair of shoes, books, or whatever was available down on the tile and walked on them in fear of touching the tile, like if I did I would immediately get sick. I was in major culture shock mode.

The next morning, one of the first things we did was to visit the president of the branch Elder Wilson and I were assigned to work in. We sat down with this wise older man, and he began to speak to us. He was speaking the Uruguayan form of Spanish, called Castellano (pronounced Casteshano). Immediately my throat sunk to my chest. I couldn't make out one word he said. He would look at me and say something. I would nod, pretending like I understood him, but he knew very well I had no idea what he was saying. For all I knew, he could have been speaking to me in Chinese. I remember thinking, *So much for thinking being able to communicate with Uruguayan people would be easy. This Uruguayan Spanish doesn't resemble anything I was taught in the missionary training center or anywhere.* I knew right then and there that I had a long way to go to communicate with the people of Uruguay and to adjust to my new surroundings.

The first few weeks in Uruguay, my trainer made sure learning the language and adjusting to the culture would be like a baptism by fire for me. On one of my first Sunday nights in Uruguay, Elder Wilson decided to team me up with another newbie (Lance Hydric) and send us out on our own while he and Lance Hydric's companion stayed back and ate ice cream and planned for the week. We had a handful of Books of Mormon and were told to head to the midtown plaza, where everybody in that town hung out, and preach the good word and give out the Books of Mormon to anyone who wanted one. With the zeal of two puppy dogs, Elder Hydric and I headed out to preach the good word.

Since neither he nor I could speak the language except for the basics, this night became a defining moment in my life on many different levels, as a missionary, person, and athlete. As we arrived to the plaza, we noticed it was the place to be, since it was packed with people. Kids were playing and dancing, and most of all there were families sitting around drinking the customary drink in Uruguay, mate. Elder Hydric and I spotted a young family walking right at us. We stopped them and began to attempt to speak to them. In the middle of what we were saying, they all broke out laughing and pointed at us like we were some traveling comedy show. We looked at each other, taking what we were saying and ourselves very seriously, and felt humiliated. After they began to attempt to speak to us in a mockery form of English, we extended a Book of Mormon to them and nodded. They took it, and that was the last we saw of them. Our puppy-dog-like zeal was tested time and time again as we attempted to strike up conversations and preach the good word that night. It was the most humiliating thing I had experienced up until that point in my life. Our Spanish was so bad, the people couldn't help but laugh at us, and the younger generations made sure we knew how goofy we sounded by laughing and pointing in our faces.

Tired and almost broken, we needed to head back to reunite with our original companions as it was getting close to our curfew. On our way back, coming right at us with a calm stroll was another family that would be very convenient to speak to. With some doubt and a little fear, I asked Elder Hydric if he wanted to stop and attempt to talk to this family. His response was simple yet profound. He said, "I am not afraid." I thought, *I agree with that. We have already been through the worst. What else is there to fear?* Away we went again, fumbling along, trying as hard as we could to preach the good word. The result was the same as before that night. We really couldn't communicate with them, making for an awkward exchange.

After about nine months of battling on a daily basis the humiliation of being made fun of and getting some pretty confused looks because of my struggles with the Uruguayan Spanish language, I finally started getting to the point to where I began to speak Spanish with ease. Because of the no-fear attitude that was very deeply encoded in my being early on in my mission experience with Elder Lance Hydric, I didn't shy away from opening my mouth and attempting to speak Spanish, even though at times what came out of my mouth didn't make sense or sounded funny. Eventually that attitude led to me learning the Spanish language. Since then, I have kept developing my ability to speak Spanish and learned to speak it well enough to eventually be hired as a color analyst for Fox Deportes, the most popular Spanish speaking sports channel in the United States. For the first time in the history of the United States of America, I was able to be a part of the first ever all-Spanish telecast of Super Bowl 48. Just like when I competed as an athlete on the field or court, I rose to the challenge of the competitive moment, which was tackling the process of learning to speak Spanish. If it wasn't for my competitive spirit to go toe to toe with such a difficult challenge without backing down, I may have never been able to fully learn the language as I did.

I realized really quickly as a missionary that even though I had put on hold for two years my competitive lifestyle as an athlete, I would still have to compete ferociously like never before, just in a different setting and in a different way. In light of coming to this realization, I finally understood a little golden nugget of wisdom one of my impressionable high school coaches, Bubba O'Neil had shared with me. He said "Sports is life with the volume turned up". At the time in my life when Bubba had imparted this wisdom to me, I was too naive and inexperienced to fully understand what he was trying to say. After taking on the difficult task of learning the language and assimilating to a foreign culture in Uruguay, I now could fully grasp what Bubba meant.

He meant that through the duration of an athletic contest, we are going to experience many of the same challenges, emotions, successes and failures as we will in our daily lives, along with learning the coping skills to allow us to appropriately manage such intense emotional swings as we strive to rise to the challenges presented by the competitive moment. The difference is, that on the field of competition, this all happens in a condensed amount of time. For example, throughout the duration of a football game that lasts three hours, you most likely will experience a roller coaster ride of emotions that range from the highs of success, to the lows of failure. In our daily lives it may take someone years to experience those same contrasting emotions of success and failure. Although, on the field of competition the process of confronting and overcoming such diverse emotions of success and failure happens in a relatively concentrated amount of time, the way to attain lasting success both in our daily lives and on the field of competition is the same. We must continually make a conscious choice to approach any challenge that may come our way with an attitude that regardless of how daunting of a task we may face, we will not be denied our desired outcome.

I experienced this firsthand as a missionary in Uruguay. At that time for me, my field of competition was in a foreign country: Uruguay. I was competing against the intimidating challenges of the natural fear of being made fun of, and the humiliation that came with the process of learning a new language and adjusting to my new surroundings. I faced these challenges with the same competitive mindset as if I were competing in an intense game of football. Because the reality is, no matter where we are or what we do, just because we are not in a field, court, or course to compete as athletes, we all have to compete, even if at the very least to step outside our comfort zone and go toe to toe with a task that from the onset may be intimidating or against our nature.

4

WHEN YOU SEE WHO YOU ARE, YOU WILL SEE WHO YOUR OPPONENT IS

Life as a missionary was in stark contrast to the competitive life I had experienced in the first nineteen years of my life. I was going to have to carry myself very differently. Previously, my emotions had run wild. I had a short fuse. At times my temper would get the best of me. Especially in the heat of competition, any sign of possible defeat triggered a rage inside of me. In those competitive situations, that rage would be directed at my opponent. I feared defeat and the feeling of being abased that goes with it. For that reason, I had no respect toward my opponents. The only thing that mattered was coming out victorious and preserving my successful self, even if it meant mistreating those I competed against.

On the other hand, as a missionary, I entered a world where everyone was to be esteemed to the highest. I learned that the worth of souls is great in the sight of God, no matter who they are. My fellowmen were to be respected to the highest degree because of their divine potential for who they could become and what they could achieve. Because of this, I knew I should display my respect for them through the way I treated them. Ultimately, the way I treated my fellowman would be a reflection of how I would treat God if I were in His presence: just like it says in the following passage: "Inasmuch as ye have done it unto one of the least of my brethren, ye have done it unto me" (Matt. 25:40).

Brady while on his mission in Uruguay in 1998.

THE TRUE SPIRIT OF COMPETITION

Additionally, moral values such as honesty and integrity were principles that embodied a missionary's life. Without them, a missionary life's objective would be compromised because one's credibility is lost. No one would take a selfish or dishonest missionary seriously, so playing outside of the rules was not an option.

In the early stages of my mission experience, I began to visualize my future self. Basically, I had three options of who I could become. One, I could live out my mission experience and go through the motions of teaching and preaching Christian principles. Then after my time as a missionary ended, I could revert back to living life as I had lived prior to my mission experience. Two, I could avoid highly competitive situations altogether, like playing football. Or three, I could find a way to still compete passionately but at the same time uphold high honorable standards of Christian principles.

The problem with reverting back to my old premission life was that I am a person who strives for constant progression. At this point I had come so far as a person. I was on a trajectory that was leading me to higher places. I felt I was progressing as a person like never before in my life. I wasn't about to stop that momentum, so regressing back to my life before my mission was not an option. At this time I didn't trust that I could be disciplined enough in the heat of competition to stand for moral Christian values. By default, that left me with really only one option moving forward: I needed to strongly consider giving up my pursuit of a football career altogether after my mission was over. If I couldn't practice what I preached at all times, especially in the heat of competition, then I felt I would be taking an enormous step backward. I was at a crossroad, ready to leave my dream of football and its amped-up, competitive lifestyle behind. I was already going to leave it for two years, so I rationalized it wouldn't be that hard to leave it for good. I was torn between giving up my lifelong dream of playing football at BYU and in the NFL and wanting to put myself in situations that were conducive to treating others respectfully. I clearly needed some guidance, so I did what I knew to be the greatest way to find direction in life—I prayed.

I knelt down with an open heart, ready to do whatever I felt prompted to do. I asked God if I should give up something I loved—to compete as a football player. Not all prayers are answered immediately, but this one was. The answer came as clearly as if someone were standing right next to me and personally instructing me on what to do. I was impressed to continue to pursue my football ambitions. The only thing that had yet to be answered was how I was going to be able to compete with all my heart and still hold true to the high benchmark of moral Christian standards—standards I was now encouraging the people of Uruguay to live. My new challenge was how to find a way to interlace the two contrasting worlds into one.

After wrestling with this idea for a time, I had an epiphany that forever changed the way I viewed competition. I was searching for the answer to how I could compete against my opponents with the love, passion, and conviction I had in the past and in a way that enabled me to respect them. What triggered the epiphany was an interesting situation among the missionaries.

At the crack of dawn, the roosters signaled it was morning with their loud cackle. I checked to see what time it was: 5:30 a.m. I thought to myself, *Yes, another hour of sleep!* As I placed my head back on the pillow, it was hard to fall back to sleep, not only because of the continuous cackling of the roosters outside of our bedroom window but also because today was going to be P-day or preparation day. This day for a missionary was our day of rest. It wasn't exactly a day of rest in the sense that you would just lounge around taking naps and doing nothing, although you could if you wanted to. It was a day of rest in the sense that it was a day where

THE TRUE SPIRIT OF COMPETITION

you wouldn't be following the rigorous schedule you would follow the other six days of the week.

During the rest of the week, you would wake up at 6:30 a.m. and constantly be going all through the day studying, planning, and walking from one appointment to another preaching the good word until 9:30 p.m. Preparation day was more of a day of getting your haircut, cleaning your apartment, dropping off your laundry, and most exiting of all—playing. I mean playing hard. On preparation day we would play all sorts of sports, like soccer, baseball, football, and basketball. We would play card games, and board games. When I received a package from my parents with taped BYU or NFL football games, I would use the preparation day to sit down and watch these games. Preparation day to a missionary is an exciting day.

On this particular preparation day, since I was new, I was going to allow my more-experienced companion (Elder Wilson) to plan out the day. He had planned for us to stop by the church first thing in the morning, where all of the missionaries in the area would meet up to play card games. Today was going to be an Uno tournament. As Elder Wilson and I entered into the room to where these intense games of Uno were being played, you could feel the tension in the air. All of a sudden one missionary blurted out, "Uno!" indicating that he only had one card left. Since the object of the game is to see who could rid themselves of all of their cards first, the missionary with only one card was on the verge of victory. You could see the concern on his opponent's face that he was in a pickle as he had a handful of cards. After laying down one of the many cards he had, the missionary left with only one card wound up, and like a tomahawk slam-dunk, he slammed down his final card to win the game. He then proceeded to do a victory dance, rubbing the victory in the face of his opponent.

Relating to this missionary's unsportsmanlike behavior, I thought, *That had to be the most intense Uno game I have ever witnessed.* All of a sudden, interrupting the very intense competitive environment, one of the missionaries who was a member of our leadership group made the comment that we were only allowed to play games that were noncompetitive. I thought that was an odd way of playing games because the whole purpose of engaging in any game was to win, right?

I was relatively new to my mission, and I began to think that the noncompetitive rule would be very challenging to follow for two whole years—not only for me but also for anyone. I also thought it was a rule that was unrealistic since everyone competes, if not against someone else then at least with themselves. I was shocked to think that there was a rule against competition, like competing was a sin. I eventually learned that in our area, there had been an ongoing problem over the last few months of unsportsmanlike behavior that led to some conflicts among missionaries following the sports or games that were played on preparation day. After hearing that, I figured competition wasn't the problem. It was the way competitive situations were being handled that was the problem. The noncompetitive rule was implemented to help keep the peace among missionaries. After all, any kind of conflict or fight would put a wrench in our missionary objectives. We were there to preach the gospel of Jesus Christ, goodwill toward men, charity, and doing service for others.

It was interesting to me that the very thing I was having a hard time trying to figure out was something these other missionaries were also struggling with. I wasn't the only one weighed down with feelings of how one could possibly adhere to the high moral standards and values of Christianity but at the same time be able to compete vigorously. I was convinced that there had to be a way we could all get along yet be able to compete against one another.

THE TRUE SPIRIT OF COMPETITION

At that time I still was not able to figure it out. I thought back to the kind of relationships I had with my brothers growing up and felt that it was much harder to get along with those I competed against, but it had to be possible, right?

That night I thought more deeply about what I had been wrestling with for some time. There must be a way to compete and still respect my opponent, but how? God would not have prompted me to continue to play football if He did not provide a way. From what I experienced earlier that day with the other missionaries, competing with respect toward your opponent was very difficult because even in a competition among friends who were missionaries, emotions could still escalate and get overly heated and confrontational. I continued to ponder whether anyone could truly compete with all of his or her heart, might, mind, and strength and regardless of whether he or she won or lost, still walk away peacefully with mutual respect and rapport for the opponent when the competition ended.

After a lot of thought, prayer, and deliberation, the answer to my question finally came to me while I was sleeping. I awoke and immediately wrote down my thoughts. It was so clear and yet so simple. I thought, *Why couldn't I see this before?*

The key was a flaw in how I viewed myself, which was also tied to how I viewed my opponent. I realized I was competing with the erroneous idea that my worth as a human being was reflected on the scoreboard. I felt as though I was competing for actual superiority. The false assumption was that if I won, I felt I was a better person than my opponent. When I lost, I mistakenly felt that I was inferior. I finally understood that this was the reason why I was getting so emotionally amped up in competitive situations. My self-worth was on the line. It was a big ego trip.

No wonder I had no respect for my opponents. If I lost, I blamed them for making me feel like a loser, a failure. Because

I felt threatened in this way, it was not surprising that I had no regard for the well-being of my opponents. It became clear to me why the intense emotions of competitive situations could escalate to the point of feeling hostile toward one another. If one felt that the final outcome of a game or match ultimately defined one's self-worth, I could understand why one would go so far as cheating or intentionally trying to injure one's opponent to win. No one instinctively wants to feel inferior or worthless. No one wants to be known as a failure or a loser. For that reason, the perceived threat on a personal level imposed by the opponent would have to be eliminated at all costs.

The point I was missing was that the outcome of a competition does not determine first and foremost who we are. Regardless of the outcome of any competition, we, at our core, are incredibly intelligent and capable beings with unlimited potential whose souls are great and immeasurable. A win or a loss is never going to change that.

By eliminating the personal aspect of competition and understanding that the outcome would not be a reflection of me or my opponent's self-worth, the threat imposed by my opponent disappeared, as did my defensiveness. I came to see my opponents as the source of an oppositional force that would test my strength and skill rather than personally attack my self-image. When I saw my opponents this way, competition became an impersonal experience to see how I measured up to the opponents I confronted.

For example, when we run alone, although we may think we are running as fast as we possibly can, it is not until we compete against someone in a head-to-head race that we run our fastest. This is because we now have a reference point we can measure our speed against. This is what the true spirit of competition is about—making a conscious choice to take the opposing forces we face head-on, resulting in one's highest level of performance being extracted. An opponent plays a vital role in making this happen.

Second, I came to realize that my definition of success was also off base. It dawned on me that a scoreboard doesn't determine success or failure. Success could have as many different meanings as there are people on this earth. Success is determined by how any given person performs, according to his or her expectations and derived from the person's situation. For example, if someone who has just recovered from a serious illness were to finish a half marathon, it would be a huge success for him or her to be able to compete in the race, win or lose. To those whose talents and abilities are at a level unmatched by others, it is very conceivable that not even a victory would be a measure of success if they did not play to the best of their ability. The problem was that I equated success with winning, and that meant that success was something my opponent could take away from me. I realized being successful was a choice I made regardless of outside forces. Being successful wasn't an end result but the way someone operated. That flaw in my reasoning was clearly a mistake on my part.

Because of my new outlook on competition, success became something that couldn't be snatched away from me by my opponent. Therefore, my opponents no longer posed a threat to my successful self. Instead, my opponents pushed me to dig deep and to be my most successful self possible. The responsibility of making the successful side of myself manifest was now on my shoulders alone and within my control. I could feel successful as long as I fully engaged all my senses in the present competitive moment, trying as hard as I could to come out victorious for myself and for my team. Success was obtained by simply making an inward conscious choice to rise to the challenges my opponent presented independent of anything else.

I came to understand that if the scoreboard no longer reflected my own personal success, then there was a greater purpose to competition than just winning or losing. By confronting the obstacles a competition provides, one experiences the sharpening of one's competitive will. One's skill sets, abilities, and knowledge on a holistic level become more refined. Winning was the goal but only the byproduct of the process, not the end. The end was that, in spite of whether one wins or loses, one could experience the gradual personal growth of one's being that comes from meeting head-on the struggles of the heat of competition.

Losing took on a whole new meaning. Although it is disappointing and it hurts, losing is not death. Some of the biggest improvements personally come from failing and losing. There is no true success without failure. Just ask any great competitor or champion. I saw where losing was a blessing in some cases instead of a curse. Enduring a disappointing loss reveals the flaws of your performance, which is very humbling. Thus you are more willing to learn. After a loss, the answers to the questions of what needs to be polished and honed to eventually come out victorious are more clearly visible.

Winning, on the other hand, is more about validation than anything. When one wins, one's past efforts of improving and growing are rewarded. One needs to be very careful with winning, however, because sometimes winning can lull us into a complacent sleep. We can be made to believe that there is no more need for progress or development. That is not the case. Since our potential has no bounds, there is always room to increase our level of performance. Following a great victory, our souls fill with a euphoric adrenaline rush of knowing that the struggles endured along the way were not in vain but very much a major part of the reason why we came out victorious.

In summary, I came to understand that a scoreboard no longer determined my own worth as a person or that of my opponent.

THE TRUE SPIRIT OF COMPETITION

Regardless of the outcome of a competition, our worth is beyond the scope of any label or word that could attempt to describe it. No matter what creed, race, color, ethnicity, or religion, we are all beings whose potential has no ceiling. When we begin to see the true spirit of competition as grounds for pushing our personal levels of performance to new heights, instead of a measure of our worth as a human, competition becomes more enjoyable and rewarding.

After this realization of who I was, I felt at peace. I felt comfortable, confident, and secure in my own skin, knowing that the outcome of a competition was never going to define me, resulting in an inner strength I could draw from to assist me in controlling my emotions in the heat of competition. Knowing this freed me from my insecurities and feelings of defensiveness that I had toward my opponents.

I could now compete with all the passion and zeal of my heart as I did in my youth and yet maintain strong relationships with those I competed against. It was really possible to compete fiercely and still leave the field of competition with mutual respect for my opponent because instead of imposing a threat to the very existence of my successful self, now my opponent imposed a challenge that called for the emergence of my successful self. From those lessons, instead of using competition as a way to boost my ego, I now saw competition as a way to enhance my capacity to perform and to grow closer to my true potential. After my mission would be the best time in my life to apply those things I learned when I faced my most formidable rival, my elder brother, head to head on the biggest stage of our lives: in a college football game.

5

THE FACELESS OPPONENT

Two deer cautiously meandered their way down a narrow game trail through the trees, making their way to a clearing to graze. The leaves of the trees were the vibrant red, yellow, and orange colors of fall. The sun was slowly setting behind the majestic mountains. There was no wind. It was one of the most calm and peaceful displays of nature that you could imagine. It was the calm before the storm. It was as contrasting of an environment that you could find from what I was about to enter into. I was in my hotel room gazing out the window while packing up the last of my things to catch the bus to head to Logan, Utah, and take on the Aggies of Utah State.

As I left my room and found my seat on the bus, I put on my favorite pregame music, which to many people's surprise wasn't heavy metal. It was relaxing, calm music (sometimes Enya). I started to think about what this game meant to me and my family. I began to relive what had happened in the week leading up to the game. This was one of the biggest games of my life because I was on the verge of taking on my greatest rival—the opponent who knew my every strength and weakness, as I knew his. I was getting ready to face head to head my fiercest rival: my elder brother, Casey.

When I mean face him, I mean we were literally going *mano y mano*, head to head. He played tight end, and I played at the time defensive end. The nature of these two positions was that for many plays throughout a game, the tight end would have to block one on one the opposing team's defensive end. That meant Casey and I were going to have to lock horns on more than a few occasions, just like old times. The burning question in everyone's minds who knew Casey and I was, would this head-to-head competition end up like all the others, resulting in an intense, contentious fight? All throughout the week leading up to the game, and even through the game, my parents and family members didn't know how this was going to pan out. From what I was told, both of my parents didn't show any emotion in fear of not wanting to unfairly cheer for or against either one of us. It was an awkward game for my parents especially. They were sitting on pins and needles to see how this would pan out.

During the week leading up to the game, the media made it a very intriguing story about us two brothers facing off. Although the year before Casey's and my team had faced off, Casey and I didn't meet head to head because I predominately played special teams while he played on offense. This year was very different since we would be going face to face. A funny quote that came from all of the media attention was from our mom. She was asked what she would do if Casey and I started to get into a fight on the field. She responded by saying, "I will stop the game and give both of them a spanking in front of their coaches, their teammates, and all of the fans." To say that the media wasn't having fun with this story line of two brothers facing off would be a lie.

The one thing that people who questioned how we would handle this head-to-head battle forgot was that I was a new person from the one who would instigate fights with my elder brother in the heat of competition. I had gained better control of my passion to win. I now competed from a different place than before when I was younger. Instead of competing from a place of fear of being a failure and being willing at all costs to defend the emergence of my successful self that came in the form of a victory, I now competed from a place knowing that regardless of the outcome of the competition, as long as I committed all my energy, focus, and strength and allowed my meticulous preparation to carry me to victory, I would at the very least have my abilities, skills, and knowledge heightened because of the challenge posed by my opponent. I considered that a successful outing independent of anything else.

To confirm this mind-set, two nights before going head to head with Casey, he and I had a very open and honest talk. He explained to me that if I really respected him as a brother, I shouldn't let up and I should play with the most fanatical effort as possible against him. I reciprocated that thought. I expected him to give me his utmost, top-notch effort. I welcomed it and begged for it. Because of my new outlook on competition, my desire more than anything now in competition was to be challenged every day like never before, for one end and one end only: to realize my potential as a football player. I also knew the byproduct of this approach would mean I would win a lot, both in my individual battles and as a team.

The game and our head-to-head battle not only lived up to the hype, but it was epic. Utah is the main rival of BYU rather than Utah State, but winning this game against BYU would make the Aggies of Utah State's season an immediate success. The excitement and energy at the stadium was to the caliber of a championship game. The Aggies' fan base knew this would be their shot to knock off the favorite, the BYU Cougars. They would go to almost any length to help their team to come out victorious on this early-October Friday night. Even though Utah State and BYU are not main rivals, the game still had that flair to it.

As Utah State's offense broke its huddle and approached the line of scrimmage for one of its first plays of their opening series, I gathered that number eighty-one, Casey, was coming right toward my side of the formation. *Here we go!* I thought. As he was positioning himself to get into his stance, he said with a smile, "What's up, Brady?" I responded by saying, "What's up, bro?" After the snap of the ball, our pleasantries were over.

Casey lunged out of his stance like a lion lunging to take down its prey to attempt to drive me off the ball. I responded by also explosively lunging back at him to stop his momentum. When we engaged, our helmets and pads made an explosively loud *pop!* sound that echoed through the field as we rammed into each other like two beasts of the wild battling for territory. I attempted to stay lower than him to gain an advantage and push him back to set the edge, meaning to encourage the ball carrier to run the ball inside instead of outside, which was where Casey and I were battling.

We both forcefully extended our hands and arms out, trying to grab each other's chest area. I was trying to gain separation from Casey while he was trying to grab me so he could direct me and not allow me to disengage his block if the ball carrier did make his way near us. In this situation the one who gets his hands to the chest first and stays lower usually will win this head-to-head matchup. Being a little overaggressive, as I am known to be at times, one of my hands slipped upward, and my hand unintentionally landed right in Casey's throat. Being in the ultra-focused and intense mode of wanting to carry out my responsibility, it was not until the play was over that I realized I was essentially choking him out during the play. The whistle blew to indicate the play was over, and as a defense we held the ball carrier to a minimal gain. I was able to turn the ball back inside.

THE TRUE SPIRIT OF COMPETITION

It was noticeable that in between the whistles, my elder brother and I would see each other not as brothers but as faceless opponents. He was true to his words, as was I. We were going at each other with an all-out effort to win our head-to-head battle and to help our respective teams win the game. Our head-to-head battles were going back and forth. The game on a bigger level took on that same back-and-forth nature, except instead of going back and forth play after play or series after series, this game ended up being a game of two halves.

In the first half, the Aggies of Utah State rode the emotions of the high energy and electric ambiance and dominated the first half, going up thirty-four to seven. Everything they did, they did it with more energy and determination than we did. They deserved to have dominated that half. In the second half, the momentum shifted 180 degrees. We went on a run offensively and defensively that turned the tide of the game. As a defense we shut down the Utah State Aggie offense holding them scoreless in the second half. Offensively, we found our rhythm and ripped off twenty-eight unanswered points to take the lead late in the fourth quarter thirty-five to thirty-four. With one last hope to win the game, the Aggies had to drive the length of the field with time running out.

I was tired and worn out from an emotional game that had it shares of highs and lows. My all-white uniform was covered in grass stains, blood, and dirt. I knew I had to dig deep to find a way to finish off one of the greatest comebacks in BYU history. We were going to implement a prevent defense to where we would rush only three and drop eight defenders into coverage. Since I was only one of the three rushers, I knew I would be seeing a double team.

As the ball was snapped, I leaped out of my three-point stance. I felt the guard and the tackle both looking to block me. In a split second, I took an inside track on the tackle toward the helping guard. I faked like I was going to ram right into the face of the guard. At the last second, I pulled away and ole'd him like a charging bull. I now had a clear track to the QB. He was just beginning his throwing motion as I went to get a hit on the him, trying to split him in half and make him pay. Smack! I ran through him as hard as I could. Lying on top of the QB, after hearing him grunt to brace himself for the impact of the initial hit and me landing on him, I heard a faint roar of the crowd. I stood up and reoriented myself. I saw one of our guys running with the ball. We had intercepted the ball. Game over!

I joined my teammates and celebrated a crazy and unbelievable comeback victory. Right after that I found my elder brother, Casey. Instead of ending this head-to-head competition in the same fashion as our matchups as youth, which were with haymakers and headlocks, we shook hands and hugged each other. We told each other good game. It was the first time we finished a head-to-head matchup to its end. We walked away from the field of competition that day with greater mutual respect and with a stronger bond. Instead of competition driving us apart as it did in our youth, it made us closer.

The key for us that day was that, even though we shared the bond of brothers with one another, we looked at each other in the heat of competition like faceless opponents. We saw each other as faceless opponents who would test our skill, strength, and technique in order to improve them. What allowed us to control our emotions and tunnel them toward a productive outing as two brothers facing off in an intense competition was our focus on the process of competition more than just the end result of winning or losing. Because of the process-based focus, we were able to see each other in a positive light as opponents.

The true spirit of competition was experienced that day. We both had fully invested all of our energies, focus, and strength to help our teams win. When the game clock struck zero, only one team could win, but both of us benefited from the experience.

THE TRUE SPIRIT OF COMPETITION

Brady with his older Brother Casey after having just faced off in a historic game between BYU and Utah State.

6

AN UNLIKELY OPPONENT

The bell rang. I pulled out my earplugs, took off my safety glasses, and headed over to the food truck for a little midmorning snack. I removed my greasy leather gloves. I was going to be working a full ten-hour shift. Then following the ten-hour shift, I was going to head to the weight room and train for another two hours. I needed to eat something that was going to be sustainable. I purchased myself a thick, dense oat bran muffin. Every time I took a bite of the muffin, I would get this whiff of a strong leather smell from my fingers that was left from wearing the leather gloves. The bell rang again, and back to work I went.

I returned to my station in the factory, where I would box the ladders after they had been assembled and then stack them until the stack was higher than my head. I would then transport the ladders to the storage area ready to be shipped across the world. I was chosen to do the heavy-lifting job because of my height and strength to lift hundreds of ladders a day.

This was my job that I did for five months following my return from my mission experience in Uruguay. I started in August of 2000 and worked through December of 2000. Instead of enrolling at BYU for the fall semester and beginning my clock of eligibility, the coaches decided it would be best for me to sit out the first semester so I could get myself back into playing shape. When I did get into shape, for most missionaries it took about a year to return to form, and the coaches wanted all five of my eligible years to play. In this time frame where you are not enrolled as a full-time student yet you are going to be at the commencement of the next semester, they called you a gray shirt. During this gray-shirt time, I worked a job in Wings ladder factory in Springville, Utah. My day began at a quarter to five in the morning and usually ended at half past eight in the evening following my training.

In mid-December, I left my Wings ladder factory job and headed back to my hometown of Evanston, Wyoming, to pass the holiday season with my family. While there, I continued on my strict training routine. To do my training, I would make my way to Evanston High School, my alma matter, and lift weights and run to get myself back to form.

At this time I felt in the five months after the return from my mission, I was about 90 percent back to form. I was way ahead of schedule. I was excited to be finally enrolling in BYU in the next few weeks and beginning my dream of donning the Y on my helmet as a BYU football player. I wanted to push for playing time right away. I kept pushing my training, hoping to go from feeling 90 percent back to form to maybe close to 100 percent by the time we kicked off the offseason training in January of 2001.

As I entered into my old weight room in Evanston High school, I reminisced about my days as an athlete back in high school. I remembered the hard training sessions and the great accomplishments, like winning a state football championship in 1997. It was fun to return to my old stomping grounds.

After loosening up the body, the first exercise in my routine was power cleans. It was one of my favorite lifts because it developed explosiveness that translated into power and speed on the football field. I loaded the bar gradually until I hit the target weight, which was 265 pounds. I wasn't using the safer bumper plates that allow you to just drop the bar at the top of the lift to protect your back and joints because the school didn't have them. In the first few sets, I dropped the bar with the steel metal plates. When the steel plates impacted the floor, it made a loud banging sound that echoed through the school. I noticed the loud sound of the falling weights was attracting the attention of a nearby PE class. On the last set and repetition, I decided to attempt to gradually set the weight down instead of dropping it to avoid disrupting the nearby class.

I was not only tired from the training that day, but also I was feeling the accumulative effect of fatigue after stacking ladders for ten hours a day for the last few months. I began to struggle as I attempted to set the weight down onto the ground under control. Adding to the strain, the weight was pretty heavy as I tried to lower 265 pounds of weight. I couldn't control the weight any longer. The weight folded me in half as it fell to the ground. All of a sudden, I felt and heard a pop in my back. I felt something in my back shift. It was a feeling I had never experienced before. I didn't think anything of it and kept training. For the next few days, I wondered what that pop in my back was. I didn't have any pain or impairment—yet.

A few days following this weightlifting incident, my father and my two brothers headed to the beautiful Rocky Mountain range in Utah to enjoy the fresh and soft powder by doing some skiing. As I started to slide on my skis for the first time in six years, I felt like I had never left the slopes. It was like riding a bike. My father and two brothers and I were finally together for the first time in four years. It would be another two years before we were all together again because of missions. My younger brother would be heading out to Ecuador in a few weeks, so we wanted to celebrate being together. We hit the slopes at Snowbird to enjoy a little male bonding.

After an intense day of skiing, we took off our ski gear to head back home. As I removed my ski boots, just like I recalled every other time I skied before, my feet felt numb because of the tightness of the ski boots. About an hour or two later, in my left foot, that numbness persisted. I thought, *That is unusual. I don't remember my foot staying numb for that long after skiing.* I was baffled.

The following day I continued with my training, still with numbness in my foot. I was now experiencing major low back pain, and my left leg started to shut down—I mean literally shut down. In a pick-up basketball game, I was trying to play defense, and every time I would try to change direction off of that left leg, I would collapse to the ground. After that happened a few times, I knew I had a serious injury to deal with.

Upon my return to Provo, Utah, to begin not only my schooling but to live my childhood dream playing for the BYU Cougar Football team, one of the first things I did was go and get this low-back issue checked out by the orthopedic surgeon. I was evaluated for just ten seconds by the orthopedic surgeon because of how easy it is to diagnose a disc injury. The loss of feeling in my left foot and the loss of strength in that same leg were the usual indicators of a herniated disc.

From what the trainer had told me, a number of football players currently and formerly on the team had that same injury. Some never played again and some did recover but never fully returned to their preinjury form. My prospects were looking pretty dim. Had my career just ended before it began? Had my dream of donning that Y on my helmet just vanished in one instant? Oh, I don't think so!

As I submitted my paperwork to get a MRI scan to see the extent of the injury, the secretary to the head football trainer, feeling sorry for me, said, "I am so, so sorry that this happened to you." I thought in my head, *What happened? Did someone just die of the plague, or did I just get introduced to my opponent for the next few months? I think the latter.* I immediately responded with bewilderment to her pity and asked, "Do you think this is the end for me and my football career?" With a sad face trying to be a source of reality of what I was dealing with, she nodded yes. I snapped back at her, "Oh no, this is just the beginning. I will be back better than ever, I promise." Now she felt even sorrier for me, thinking I was not only looking at a potentially career-ending injury even before my career started, but on top of that, I was delusional.

The diagnosis introduced me to my opponent for the next few months of the recovery process. It was a herniated disc. It was bulging out and touching a nerve that was causing the weakness in my leg and numbness in my foot. The first form of treatment was to shut it down for two weeks straight, doing no physical activity. I would combine the rest time with a packet of extra-strong anti-inflammatories. We hoped the rest and the medicine would cause the swelling in the disc to go down. In theory, if the bulge in the disc went down, it wouldn't be touching my nerve, and the feeling in my foot and strength in my leg would return. If that didn't work, then I would have to go under the knife and have my herniated disc surgically repaired. At that time, having surgery on my back could have been either career ending or I wouldn't have been the same athletically afterward. Avoiding surgery was my number one priority.

Every step I took, the smell of body odor intensified. The

humidity in the air of the hall way increased with every footstep. The pounding of weights and loud music echoed through the building. As I entered into the weight room, I beheld an energy that is reminiscent of a beehive. Both men and women athletes were moving from one lifting station to another with high amounts of enthusiasm.

I stopped and leaned on the railing of a stair climber and watched all the activity. The urge to drop my backpack and join them was so strong that as I fought against the urge, my legs began to shake. Those athletes who knew me looked at me, confused, as they wondered why I hadn't joined them. One of the football players I hadn't met yet came up to me. With the curiousness of a cat, he began to question what I was doing.

He asked, "Are you a walk-on thinking about joining the football team?"

(A walk-on is someone who isn't offered a scholarship to play football but has to pay his own way.) Not really wanting to elaborate on my situation because every last bit of my brain energy was being allocated to fighting against my urge to lift weights, I responded with a short response by saying, "No, I am on scholarship."

He asked, "Well, why aren't you working out with us?"

Now this would make at least the hundredth time having to explain that I was injured. I impatiently said, "Bro, I have an injury that I am waiting to heal up."

He said, "Okay". Then he walked away.

Not wanting to continue to torture myself, I left the weight room and headed back to my apartment. On the way there, over and over again, I had to refrain from going from a normal walk to a full-out sprint. Everywhere I looked, whether it was a hill, a tree, or just even a case of stairs, I felt this impulse attempting to lure me to run up the hill, climb the tree, or run up the stairs. I had so much pent up energy and such a strong desire to train that I was on the verge of using all that stored-up energy. Unfortunately, that would have compromised my recovery process, and I surely would have had to go under the knife and surgically repair the disc, thus greatly jeopardizing my future as a football player.

What I would do was take a deep breath, compose myself, and remind myself that if I wanted to have the best chance possible of defeating this herniated disc, I would have to allow the anti-inflammatories combined with the rest to do their job. My desire to defeat this ailment was stronger than that draw trying to allure me to workout.

I had now been out of commission for a week. Over a week's span, I hadn't done any sort of physical activity. It seemed like every morning I would wake up and the feeling in my foot would slowly, incrementally make its way back, as would the strength in my leg. At this rate, I knew that if I let the full two weeks pass, we would make it through what I believed was the hardest part of the recovery process—doing absolutely no physical activity for two full weeks.

After the two weeks of pure rest and taking the full pack of medicine, I began to get full feeling in my foot back again, and my leg didn't seem as weak. It worked! Instead of having to go under the knife, I was able to avoid surgery altogether.

The first part of the competition against a very challenging opponent, my herniated disc, had just come to an end, with me taking an early lead. It turned out to be the most challenging part of the whole recovery process because it has been, and still is, by far more difficult to rest and do nothing than it is to be active. There were times during that two-week stretch when I thought I was going to go crazy. But fortunately I stuck it out. I had won that battle, but the war was far from over.

Finally, even though I wasn't feeling 100 percent like I had set out to be back six weeks earlier when I went home for the holidays, I was just happy that I was cleared to finally take part in team workouts. No longer was I working out as a gray shirt. No longer was I trying to get clearance just to participate with the team because of the herniated disc in my back. I was as excited as a kid on Christmas morning. I was now able to lift weights with the team and slowly get myself back to form.

As with any nerve issues like mine, there is some damage sustained to the nerve. Since this nerve dealt with my left leg and foot, I almost had to reteach the nerve how to fire correctly and reteach myself how to use that left leg again. For about a month, we had been lifting weights, but we hadn't gone out to the field and run around doing football movements yet. I mostly did upper-body lifts still, trying to allow my back to fully heal. I was slowly regaining strength and function in my left leg, but I had a long way to go to become fully healthy again. I noticed this the first time we worked out on the field.

It was an overcast, cooler afternoon in February. As I walked out onto the BYU football practice field for the first time since my days of coming to the summer camp back in high school, I was in football heaven. I was as excited as a horse who had been pent up in a barn all winter and the doors of the barn just opened for spring. That excitement was going to get tested very soon.

Our planned workout was to run ten 110-yard sprints and then go and do position work with our position coaches. I figured that these 110-yard sprints would be easy. After getting loosened up, we lined up to run the ten 110-yard sprints. As soon as the whistle blew to start the sprint, I shot out of the blocks like an Olympic sprinter. I crossed the finish line ten yards in front of the next player. Then twenty seconds after finishing the first one, we would run another. Twenty seconds later, the whistle blew again. I shot out of there and sprinted that one like the first one, but this time I could feel my lungs burning. My legs were starting to get heavy.

THE TRUE SPIRIT OF COMPETITION

The wet grass of the field started to seem like quicksand. Twenty seconds later, the whistle blew again for the third one. Trying as hard as I could just to stay even with everybody, I was now losing major ground with every stride. I was ten yards behind the next player when we finished. My left leg was lagging, and my back was locking up.

I ground out the next seven in the same fashion. My lungs were on fire. My heart was beating as hard as it possibly could. I was seeing stars because of the lack of oxygen flowing to my brain. My legs almost gave way with every step as I walked around, trying to cool down from the run. My linebackers coach, Coach Schmidt, called us over. We jogged over. For me to just jog over to him seemed to be as taxing as running one of those 110-yard sprints.

To add insult to injury, as I was trudging over to see my position coach, I passed by our defensive line coach at the time. His name was Tom Ramage. He heckled me by saying, "Poppinga, you were looking like a jackrabbit out there." Having a hard enough time just making my way over to be with my position group, I couldn't understand how I looked like a jackrabbit since I was bringing up the rear on all but one of those 110-yard sprints. Jackrabbits are usually known to being fast and shifty. Maybe he was referring to the hitch in my step because of my locked back and messed-up left leg. On this occasion the herniated disc got the best of me and evened up the score. But we had a long way to go.

As spring ball began in March, it was the time to show the coaches what they were getting after having invested a scholarship in me. With my back still bothering me, I struggled through spring practice. The first impression is usually the most important. This time it was no different. I played okay during spring, but I was perceived by my coaches as a player who needed a lot more time to develop. Even after fully recovering from my herniated disc, when I felt as fast and as strong as ever, that perception stuck with me.

Right before the beginning of the 2001 season, my head coach at the time, Coach Gary Crowton, sat me down, trying to convince me to redshirt. My thought process was that whether I red shirted or not, in four more seasons I was heading off to the NFL, so he might as well just play me and forget my redshirt. I was turning twenty-two that year anyway. I wasn't getting any younger. The herniated disc now took the lead.

All through the season I hardly saw the field as a positional player except in clean-up time. I pretty much just played special teams. Additionally, just as I was getting used to playing my position of desire, middle linebacker, Coach Schmidt, who was not only my position coach but also the defensive coordinator, pulled me aside and wanted me to switch positions to defensive end. Again, it was confirmed that they didn't think much of me as a player because an ongoing theme for many linebackers the coaches were giving up on was they were essentially switched to defensive end or the trash pile as it was called. I didn't let that slow me down. I figured that now my focus would turn to becoming a dominant defensive end. By the end of my freshman year, the prospects of how my college football career would pan out were still up in the air. I did know one thing: my new position of defensive end fit my personality to a T. Now all I needed to was to keep believing in myself.

During the 2002 season, my sophomore year's off season, I was fully recovered from my herniated disc. The proof of that was during sprint practice. In that offseason the former defensive line coach retired and a new one came into town who was perfect for me. His name is Steve Kaufusi. He began teaching me techniques and pass rush moves that would take my intense mentality and translate it into production on the football field. I listened and implemented every bit of coaching advice he shared with me, trusting that he knew what it took to be a great defensive end.

THE TRUE SPIRIT OF COMPETITION

That spring practice it all came together for me and ignited my football career. That realization took place during our first team scrimmage during spring. In one series, I ran over a 350-pound offensive tackle for a sack. I blew past the same guy for another sack. On a play downfield, I ran down a running back from behind. My play was dominant. I knew I would become the player I had dreamed of. I then took the lead away from my herniated disc and didn't look back.

On testing week, I was able to measure how far I had come from when I had that disc bulge and hit my nerve, putting me back a bit. I ran my forty that week in a 4.5 weighing around 255 pounds. Not many guys in the world that big can run that fast. I know had quantifiable proof that I had not only put myself in position to be a dominant player but that I had also defeated that herniated disc injury once and for all. To this day I have had no issues with my back.

The perception of the coaches changed too. After being questioned if I was going to be a player for the BYU football program, I now was seen in a different light. To confirm this, following a very disappointing loss during the first part of that same 2002 season Coach Schmidt, the defensive coordinator and my former linebacker coach, addressed the defense. He read off my stats. I had accumulated a stat line of five tackles, two sacks, three tackles for loss, and two forced fumbles. It was a dominant effort. After reading off my stat line, he declared to the whole defense, "If we had a few more Brady Poppingas, we would never lose a game."

From that point forward, I became first team all-conference three years in a row at three different positions. In 2005, after transitioning back to playing linebacker, I was drafted in the fourth round to the Green Bay Packers as a linebacker. So much for not being able to play linebacker. That became my position for my whole eight-year career as a professional.

My competitive spirit pushed me through this situation of taking on a major setback, such as the herniated disc injury. Because I focused in on the herniated disc like an opponent, every level of my being was tested. Rising to these tests over time with perseverance and self-belief brought me to higher levels of performance and achievement. I can honestly say that without that herniated disc, I highly doubt that the achievements I was able to attain would have been possible. This wouldn't be the last time I was injured with an injury that would be considered a career-threatening one. I ended up tearing my ACL twice throughout my NFL career. In both cases, I handled the situation like I did with this one—as a competition with my injury. Driven by my competitive spirit, battling through these challenges resulted in vast knowledge gains, greater self-confidence, and an even stronger spirit. I was challenged like no other, but by facing these challenges with optimism—some may call it delirium—I was able to come out the other side better than when I went in. That is the essence of the true spirit of competition.

7

CAN YOU LOSE AND STILL FIND SUCCESS?

At five in the morning, the alarm clock erupted with the most annoying and high-pitched buzzing sound that it almost caused me to fall out of bed. My heart was beating so fast that it felt like it was going to jump out of my chest. I began to sweat profusely. I was dazed and confused at what time of day it was, since the sun had yet to rise and it was pitch black outside. As I cleared the cobwebs of sleep from my head, I got on my clothes and made my way to my car parked out in front of my house. As I opened the door to leave my house, the cold wind and blowing snow smacked me right in the face like I had been sucker-punched. The blowing snow on my face felt like rubber bands snapping me. I fought through the cold wind and the sideways-blowing snow. I cleared the snow off of my car's windshield and started it up. Thank goodness it ignited. I then made my way to the BYU football facilities.

As I pulled into the facility's half-empty parking lot, the only other people there were the security guards and my teammates. We all were making our way on this early, frigid February morning to start our first day of spring practice for the 2003 football season. Practice started at 6:00 a.m. sharp. We had to have eaten breakfast, put our pads on, and be ready to go by 5:45 a.m. That was because that was when we as a defense would head out to the practice field for our pre-practice work. This was before the indoor facility was built, so all of our practices were outside, making our practice environment subject to the weather of the day. Since it was in late February in Provo, Utah practicing in the snow and frigid air was our practice environment.

Many people asked, "Why in the world would you practice football at six o'clock in the morning?" I was one of these people. I always had the philosophy that God did not intend for football to be played in pads any time before eight in the morning. The body and the mind just weren't awake enough yet. We practiced at this insane hour in the morning because our head coach, Gary Crowton, wanted to ensure that everyone could make spring practice. Many of the guys had classes that conflicted with our regular practice time in the afternoon, so Coach Crowton found a time when there wouldn't be any schedule conflicts. That time happened to be at the crack of dawn.

Anybody who wanted to have a chance to play this year on defense knew they had to show up to these practices on time and ready to roll. That was because we had a new defensive coordinator in town—Bronco Mendenhall. He was all business. When Bronco was introduced to the team, Coach Crowton said, "We would like to welcome the newest member to our staff, Coach Bronco Mendenhall." Coach Mendenhall did not even crack a smile. Upon his arrival he made it very clear that anything you did previous to him being there was great but would not factor into whether you saw the field this up and coming year. Essentially all spots were open.

My first interaction with the Bronco was an exchange in the hallway of the football offices. Me being Mr. Casual, to me everyone was my bro, dude, man or buddy. As I saw Bronco, this blond-haired, young, sharp-looking dude I had heard loved to surf, in my mind I envisioned the perfect nickname to call him would be for surely dude or bro. As we passed in the hall, we each looked at each other.

He said to me, "How you doing?"

I responded by saying, "What's up, bro?"

Bronco immediately stopped in his tracks. With a slow turn and with a stoic Clint Eastwood gaze and voice, he said, "It's Coach to you." Without saying anything else, he turned and carried on his way. Although Bronco and I remember some details of that exchange differently, the one thing we both remember crystal clear is that Bronco came to town not for fun and games but for business. His business was putting out on the field the most fanatical, high-energy, fundamentally sound defense in the nation. To accomplish that, he had some very creative and extremely challenging coaching strategies.

One of Bronco's most famous and challenging drills to see who was willing to play with this high-energy, fanatical style was called the pursuit drill. It was a drill that weeded out the weak of heart. It tested recall, conditioning, and attention to detail while being deathly tired. If you made it through this drill displaying good conditioning, toughness, speed, and attention to detail, you earned a huge amount of respect from Bronco. This drill weighed so heavily on the evaluation of each player that we would study film of the previous day's pursuit drills to see who was in the right place mentally, physically, and spiritually. The drill itself was intimidating. As a defense, as we made our way out to the practice field for our pre-practice session at a quarter to six in the morning, butterflies worked themselves up in our stomachs knowing what we were about ready to put our bodies, minds, and spirits through during the pursuit drill. I remember our starting middle linebacker stopping midway out to the practice field, and because of the anxiety he was feeling, ripping off his helmet and vomiting in the grass to the side of the walkway. We hadn't even started practice yet. That shows how intimidating that one drill could be.

The pursuit drill started with the first-team defense lining up on the sideline in a sprinter's stance. As soon as Bronco blew the whistle, you would sprint out to assume your respective positions on the field. For the cornerback and safeties who had to run to the other side field, it was extra brutal. If Bronco felt that you as a group didn't run as fast as you could or if he just wanted to test you, he would make you sprint out again and again until he gave you the okay.

As soon as we all got lined up, Bronco would grab a stick that had a football connected to it on the other end. He would a call a certain defense that would indicate what responsibilities we were to carry out at the snap of the ball. Since he loved to blitz most of the time, he usually would call a blitz. He would do a cadence to see if he could draw the defensive lineman or blitzing linebacker offsides. He then would pull the stick, emulating the snap of the football. Those who were the rushers had to explode upfield toward Bronco for five yards. The other defenders who formed the coverage had to drop to their respective zones. Then, Bronco would fake like he was throwing the ball to one side of the field, you had to immediately turn and run in that direction as fast as you possibly could. To that side, there was a player who would then run down the sideline toward the end zone, mimicking an offensive player running the football. We had to chase that mock runner with proper angles and again with fanatical effort.

THE TRUE SPIRIT OF COMPETITION

While we were pursuing this mock runner, every so often Bronco would blow the whistle, which meant we had to flop onto the ground, hit our chests, and abruptly get back on our feet and reaccelerate to pursue the mock ball carrier. Twenty to thirty yards downfield, he had some orange cones set up. Every single one of us defenders had to run all the way through the cones without slowing down and to the outside of the cones. Again, if you're running from the opposite side of where Bronco pointed, you had a long way to go to get to the outside of those cones. After the first team went, then went the second team and so on, until every defender had had their chance. If only one player on any of the teams didn't follow through with every one of the aforementioned requirements, Bronco wouldn't say who it was or what the infraction was. All he would say was, "Again." We had to do it either until Bronco felt it was done to perfection or until he was satisfied.

You had no idea when the drill was going to end. There were times at the beginning of spring practice when we did this drill for forty-five minutes before Bronco was satisfied. Oh, by the way, this was the first drill of practice. After doing pursuit drills to start things off, the rest of practice was all about survival mode because generally there was nothing left in the tank after doing pursuit drills. You would be gassed.

Bronco's objective was to see if he could break our minds and our spirits. Once he felt he had broken us enough, he started to build us back up. It was like those old horse-training tactics. Since Bronco had vast experience working this training technique on horses with positive results, he used it on football players with equally as successful outcomes. He wanted to create the most challenging practice environment known to man so that, in his words, "Playing in the games would seem easy compared to what we did in practice."

We as players weren't the only ones who practiced with a

fanatical effort. Bronco was the type of guy who wanted to lead by example. If you watched any practice conducted by Bronco, you would notice that he too was running up and down the field, encouraging, teaching, and guiding his players every step of the way. On one of these early-morning spring practices, Bronco was starting to get a little sick. Maybe it was because in frigid temperatures and sideways-blowing snow, he was wearing shorts and a sweatshirt instead of snow pants, snow boots, and a heavy coat. But who knows?

Bronco would never ask us to do something he wouldn't be willing to do himself. He wanted us to be tough and fight through discomfort, so even though he was sick, he fought through it as though nothing was bothering him. At an instructional portion of practice where Bronco was going over fundamentals and the intricacies of the defense, spit was flying from his mouth like a sprinkler. One glob of spit landed right on his chin. My attention shifted away from what he was telling me to this glob of spit just sitting there. *If I were in his shoes, I would want someone to warn me about a glob of spit sitting on my chin*, I thought.

I interjected into his coaching points and said, "Coach, Coach, I can't take this anymore—you have a huge glob of spit on your chin."

He stopped, wiped his face, looked at us, and said with his Clint Eastwood type voice, "It's part of the deal." He picked up right where he left off. I realized then that Bronco not only taught a fanatical, high-energy, and tough defense, but he embodied it.

By the time spring ball ended, every one of us defenders knew the standard. The majority of us accepted this, and we became a defense that started to have a swagger about us, knowing that any challenge we faced during the season, no matter what it was, would pale in comparison to what we had to endure during these early-morning spring ball practices. As a team we were optimistic about the 2003 season and felt very confident taking on what was one of the toughest schedules in BYU history. We had on tap Georgia Tech, the number-one-ranked USC Trojans, Stanford, and nationally ranked Boise State as our nonconference schedule. Our bitter rival, the Utes of Utah, were emerging as a national powerhouse, with Urban Myer as their coach. We knew we were going to have to play the way Bronco had trained us to have a successful year.

The 2003 season began on a high note as we were able to beat a visiting Georgia Tech team that boasted what many thought had the all-time-best wide receiver to ever come out of high school. I think that prediction was pretty accurate. His name is Calvin Johnson. The next game we faced the top-ranked USC Trojans. They had a plethora of top NFL picks and multiple future Heisman Trophy winners. They were so stacked talentwise the backup quarterback, Matt Cassel, who never started one game in college for USC, ended up being drafted in the NFL and eventually became a solid starter for a number of NFL teams.

After spotting them three easy early touchdowns, we gained our composure and controlled the game until about five minutes to go in the fourth quarter. Bronco's smothering, deceptive defense was giving USC offensive coordinator Norm Chow and star QB Matt Leinart major problems. With five minutes to go in the game down eighteen to twenty-one, the wheels fell off, and USC scored two more touchdowns to finish us off.

That was how both the 2003 and 2004 seasons went for us. We had moments as a team when we would play toe to toe with the best. Then there were other moments when we played terribly. We ended up with a combined record in those two years of nine and fourteen. This was not up to the standards of BYU football. The administration at BYU decided to make a change at the head coaching position.

Gary Crowton was fired. Many of us defenders thought Bronco should be given a hard, long look and eventually the head coaching job. We knew how gifted he was as a coach and teacher. He maximized the talents of some pretty average college football players. Many from the outside looking in didn't see it that way. Even the administrators overseeing the head-coaching search couldn't see Bronco's true value as a head coach. Who could blame them? For one, Bronco's interview didn't impress because of his strong loyalty to a good friend Gary Crowton. Bronco didn't convince the administrators that he would change much of the direction the program had taken under Gary Crowton. Another factor working against Bronco was our win-loss record with him as the defensive coordinator. With wins and losses being all too often used as a measuring stick of success, how could anyone project into the future that Bronco would be successful, with a recent win-loss record as a defensive coordinator below .500?

As fate would have it, the first choice to fill the head-coach vacancy didn't work out. Again, Bronco was given another shot to communicate how he could turn the program around. With his second opportunity, he impressed enough to get the head-coaching job. What a hire it was.

Bronco has compiled over his first nine years a record of eighty-two and thirty-four. Over that time span, he has lead BYU to nine straight bowl games and two conference championships and has finished the season ranked in the top twenty-five in five of those nine seasons. That is an impressive record! Then you add in his constraints on which athletes he is able to recruit because of the honor code. That record goes from exceptional to almost unbelievable. Don't believe me—do a poll and ask anyone who knows something about college football and how challenging it is to win year in and year out. They will tell you the same. The point is that even though during his years as a defensive coordinator where

THE TRUE SPIRIT OF COMPETITION

his record was below .500, he still was having major successes. Those successes just weren't reflected on the scoreboard yet. His successes as a defensive coordinator were made manifest by those same players who he coached as a defensive coordinator over the past few years who were lobbying the administration to hire him. We knew if given the chance, he would excel as a head coach. That is because his approach, philosophies, schemes, and systems are sound.

There are many times in competitive situations where success isn't tied to a victory. Sometimes you play or do well enough to win, but you fall short and lose. The scoreboard is a limited measurement of success because it only measures, in the case of a football game, a sixty-minute time span. What happens before or after that sixty-minute clock isn't always reflected or factored in the final score. The greatest measure of success, win or lose, is the consistent, progressive steps forward that we take. But one thing is for sure: eventually, with continued patience and an unwavering faith in your processes and perseverance, the successful moments and that sixty-minute time clock will eventually sync up and you will, with time, taste the sweetness of victory. If you don't believe me then ask Bronco. But do me one favor—make sure you call him Coach.

8

WE ARE THE EXPERTS OF OURSELVES

Good thing my Tetris skills were up to par. If they hadn't been, I never would have been able to fit all my baby girl's, my wife's, and my stuff and all of our Christmas gifts into the back of our black Jeep Grand Cherokee. It was late December as we were packing up after having spent the holidays with my wife's family in sunny southern California. This Christmas was a unique one in the sense that there was no snow. The weather in California through that holiday season had clear skies. The sun was shining, with the high temperature ranging from seventy to eighty degrees. It was a nice break from the cold, snowy Christmases I had become accustomed to.

During this Christmas season, we enjoyed the wonderful food that comes with the holidays, like prime rib, turkey, brisket, and all the dressings. We enjoyed sweet desserts like pies, cakes, candy canes, and chocolate. Since I had just finished the last game of my college career over a month earlier, I was enjoying a little downtime but still staying consistent with my workout regimen. My body was sore from a killer workout I had done two days prior.

With my college football career now over, my focus was squarely placed on what was next. I was preparing myself to put on a good show of my abilities in front of all of the scouts, front office executives, and coaches at the NFL scouting combine in Indianapolis in February. After packing my Jeep to the point to where the back door was about ready to pop open, my young family and I made our way south to a small beach town called Seal Beach. My agent had rented us an apartment there because of its proximity to Athletes' Performance in Carson City, California. I was going to train there to prepare myself physically, psychologically, emotionally, and spiritually to perform at my highest level at the scouting combine in a couple of months in February.

After settling in our apartment in Seal Beach, the next day I headed to the Athletes' Performance facility, which was once named The Home Depot Center. (It has since been renamed the StubHub Center.) After arriving I met all of the prospective NFL players I had come to know from facing their teams, like Adam Seward from UNLV and Mike Patterson and Shaun Cody of USC, among many others. I was excited to work out with and compete with these guys in preparation for the scouting combine.

After getting settled, I sat down with the head trainer, who wanted me to do some baseline testing on my forty-yard dash, long jump, and some other drills. I thought, *What a waste. For the last three weeks, my diet has consisted of cakes, cookies, and candy. Not an ideal diet to be in tiptop shape. A couple of days ago I did a killer leg workout, with my legs still feeling sore and weak. This baseline testing will be no indication of where I am at.* Even though I wasn't really excited about doing this baseline testing, I told the trainer I would go through with it anyway.

Whether you agree with it or not, about 90 percent of NFL

teams weigh very heavily how fast a prospective player runs his forty-yard dash. To many teams, this is a quantifiable way of projecting an athlete's range, explosiveness, power, and general athleticism. Year in and year out, guys during the draft process either lose hundreds of thousands to millions of dollars by running slower than expected, or they make hundreds of thousands to millions of dollars by running faster than expected. The forty-yard dash was literally at this time in my career the money maker and a huge factor in how high and where I would get drafted.

As I warmed up preparing to run my baseline forty-yard dash, with my legs sore and tired every time I tried to sprint, I felt like I was running in quicksand. I laughed to myself, thinking, *I haven't been timed slower than a four-eight in the forty-yard dash in the last three years. Today I may run slower.* After warming up, the trainer made his way to the finish line, and when we signaled we were ready, he would hold out his stopwatch, ready to time us. I went first to get it out of the way. I got into my stance. My legs ached with pain, and I almost couldn't hold myself up because of how fatigued they were. I launched out of my stance as hard as I could, but I still felt no bounce in my step as I raced down the track toward the trainer at the finish line. As I passed him, he said, "Five-point-one." I laughed and thought, *I haven't run that slow of a forty since I had a herniated disc in my back about four years ago.* After about ten minutes of rest, I ran again. Another 5.1. To me it was no big deal, knowing that I was tired and not ready to run my fastest. But for the training staff at Athletes' Performance, that was the first time they had ever seen me run.

Two days later, I met with the trainers to talk about setting my goals for the up-and-coming scouting combine. The head trainer said, "You were timed a couple of days ago at five-point-one. What should we set as your goal for how fast you want to run at the combine?"

Without hesitation I said, "I'm going to run a four-point-five."

Laughing with a somewhat bewildered tone, the head trainer said, "We know you want to set your goals high. We hear this all the time, but you have to be realistic."

I laughed to myself and confidently reiterated, "I will run a four-point-five."

The head trainer, seeing that he wasn't getting anywhere with me, suggested that we call my agent to discuss the dilemma. After getting my agent on the phone, the head trainer told my agent that I had run a 5.1 forty in my baseline testing and that realistically at the combine I should be able to run a 4.8 forty. My agent then asked me with some doubt in his voice, "Brady, what do you realistically think you can run at the combine?"

I again confidently said, "A four-point-five."

Exhausted, realizing I wasn't going to change my goal or expectation, the head trainer ended the meeting by explaining to both me and my agent, "We will hold off on setting goals and see what happens."

When I left the meeting, I remember thinking, *Who is this guy to think he knows how fast I can run based off of this silly baseline test? I have run the forty numerous times. When I am at my best, which I know I will be by the time the combine arrives, I know I can run a four-five.* As we trained and the time came closer and closer to the scouting combine, all of the talk from the draft gurus like Mel Kiper was really starting to heat up. Adam Seward, who was my training partner, made sure to inform me of everything the supposed draft experts were saying about both him and me. I visited Adam at his apartment, and Adam had Mel Kiper's in-depth scouting report of all the top draft-eligible players for the 2005 draft. Curious, I decided to see what he had to say about me. To my surprise, he had a big question mark about my speed. He had estimated my forty time to be about 4.8. I thought, *Man, this is becoming a theme that my speed is being constantly questioned.*

As I was barraged with doubt about my speed from draft gurus, my trainers, and even my agent, I actually started to think that maybe they knew something I didn't know about myself. I began to think I had either lost a step, or maybe when I was timed in the forty in college, those times weren't accurate. I started to have some doubts about how well I would perform in front of all the executives, coaches, and scouts at the combine.

After a few sleepless nights, I finally broke down and spoke to my wife, Brooke, who has a master's degree in psychology. After putting our little baby down to sleep, I laid on the couch as my wife sat next to me, trying to diagnose my mental block. After I explained to her what had happened to me, she helped me sift through all of the garbage to the core of the issue. She helped remind me of one undoubtedly true reality: *I am the expert of me.* After coming to this conclusion with the help of my wonderful wife, I remember reaffirming to myself, *I know myself better than anyone. I have been with myself through the successful times, the challenging times, and everything in between. All of these other guys like the trainers, the draft gurus, and even my agent only have known me for a small fraction of time. I know what I am made of.*

After this mental breakthrough, I made a conscious choice to ignore the critics and stay confident in trusting who I was. A week before leaving for Indianapolis for the scouting combine, we did one last test of our speed to ensure we were on the right track leading up to the combine. Instead of testing the whole forty-yard dash, we only tested the first half. As I put myself in my starting stance to be tested, my mind went blank to only singularly focus on relaxing and allowing all of my training up to that point to overtake me.

Confident in my in own abilities, I relinquished my internal will to my specifically conditioned body, mind, and spirit to carry me to my desired outcome. My legs felt strong and fresh. My neurological system felt alive and active. As I lunged out of my stance, I leaped forward like a cheetah. Relaxed and feeling quick and explosive, I sprinted with long strides that with every step explosively propelled me forward faster and faster. As I passed the trainer after sprinting twenty yards, I heard the beep of the stopwatch. I made my way back to the trainer. I asked him, "What time did you get me at?" With a very impressed and somewhat surprised look, he didn't tell me my exact time. All he said was, "Fast—very fast."

Feeling confident and ready to go, we made our way to a frozen Indianapolis for the scouting combine. The NFL combine experience in many ways is compared to one big meat market. For the first two days of the three-day combine, we would parade around like a bunch of cattle being evaluated. There was a time when we were dressed in only our underwear so scouts, coaches, and team executives could see our body composition up close. We would all line up to the side of the stage lit by a spotlight. One by one we would stand in the light of the spotlight and get weighed and measured shirtless, in front of hundreds of NFL personnel, executives, and coaches. We would have in-depth tests done on our health and our bodies so the teams would have as much information as possible before making a multimillion-dollar investment. You get poked, prodded, and asked the same questions over and over again by all thirty-two teams' physicians, doctors, and orthopedic surgeons. After all of the medical procedures, you interview with individual position coaches and with teams.

At this point in the process, it was no surprise to me that many of the teams and individual coaches had the same questions about my speed as the draft gurus and the trainers leading up to the combine had. I had one meeting with two teams at once, the Denver Broncos, and my eventual linebackers coach, Winston Moss, who at the time worked for the New Orleans Saints. During the meeting they made it clear that my speed was a question mark. They explained to me that if I didn't run a fast forty yard dash, the NFL might not be for me.

In a meeting with Tony Dungy and the Indianapolis Colts, he asked me what I thought I would run my forty in. Not wanting to limit myself, I didn't give him a specific time. Instead, I confidently said, "I will run fast—very fast." Again, if I was to accept what all of the true experts thought, like the coaches and talent executives of every team, I too may have conceded that I wasn't as fast as I once thought because of all those who had questions about my speed. But because I knew who I was even more than the so-called experts, I was confident that I would set them all straight the next day, when I would finally be able to put to rest the question of my speed as the next day wasn't only the last day of the combine, but the day we would finally run our forty-yard dashes.

Waking up at 6:00 a.m. Eastern time, which would be 3:00 a.m. Pacific time, we were scheduled to run our forties at 9:00 a.m. The teams wanted to put you in a pressured situation when running your forties to get an idea of how you would perform in a somewhat pressure-packed situation. That is why they woke you up early and had you run your forty so early in the morning. When we arrived at the football field where we would be running our forties, the stands were packed on the side next to the forty-yard dash track with coaches, scouts, and executives with their own handheld stopwatches. Even though there is an official forty time, every team has their own time. It is not an objective process in timing prospective players in their forty-yard dashes. Where one team may have timed a guy at 4.7, another team may have timed the same guy at 4.5. Those two tenths of a second could mean a difference of a lot of money come draft day.

After I took in the surroundings, my focus went to activating my body and warming up like I had been doing over the past few months in training. As I went through my routine I felt quick, explosive, and awake. I could not have cared less that is was 8:30 a.m. Eastern time, 5:30 a.m. Pacific time. I was focused on doing what I had come to Indianapolis to do, and that was to show the talent evaluators who I was.

After warming up, we all lined up alphabetically. One by one each guy took their turn running their forty-yard dash. It was somewhat eerie in the sense that after guys would finish running their forty, there were no cheers, not even a peep from the coaches, executives, and scouts in the stands, as no one wanted to show their hand as to who they liked or didn't like or who they had timed who ran really fast or not. There was this eerie silence that surrounded us.

After watching all the guys go whose names were alphabetically in front of mine, it was now my turn. I confidentially strutted up to where we would start the forty-yard dash. At the starting line I saw Al Davis, the late owner of the Oakland Raiders, sitting in the second row about ten feet from where the starting line was. He was one of the many decision makers of acquiring players who was enamored with the forty-yard dash. If you run fast, in most cases on the Raiders' draft board you would really jump up the ranks.

As I positioned myself in my stance to start, everything was quiet, except for the heavy breathing of Al Davis. Redirecting my thoughts form his breath to mine, I leaped out of my stance. After somewhat stumbling, I gathered myself and ran as fast as I could through the finish line. I felt explosive and fast. But that stumble might have cost me a couple of hundredths or even tenths of a second on my time, which then could translate into hundreds of thousands of dollars lost. But because I was confident in myself, my poise didn't allow that one potential misstep to negatively affect me. My second turn came, and I ran well, this time without a stumble.

Being the impatient guy that I am and dying to know my time, I ran up to the first scout that I saw on the field and noticed that he had the official times. I asked him, "Sir, do you have our forty-yard times?" He said he did. He already knew who I was, and he said, "Five-nine and five-nine," meaning 4.59 in my first one and 4.59 in my second one! I was pumped. I knew the whole time that I could run that fast. It validated my thought that in spite of what everyone else might have thought they may have known about me, I knew myself better than anybody. Not even the true experts like the NFL coaches, executives, and scouts knew me as well as I knew myself.

Following my combine performance, my stock as a player rose. The Packers, who place a high level of emphasis on the forty-yard dash, really started to show a lot of interest in me leading up to the draft. They were impressed with my speed-to-size ratio being that I could run the forty-yard dash in the 4.5 range weighing 260 pounds. There aren't many guys in the world that big and fast at the same time. I ended up being one of only three guys who weighed over 250 pounds to run in the 4.5 range in all of the 2005 NFL draft class.

Sure enough, with the one hundred and twenty fifth pick in the 2005 draft, I received a call from the Green Bay Packers. Matt Klien, the assistant to the head coach, was the one who called me. After having me wait for a few minutes, which to an impatient person like me seemed like a couple of hours, he asked, "How would you like to play in the frozen tundra of Green Bay?" I replied by saying, "I was born and raised to play in that kind of weather, having grown up in Evanston, Wyoming."

My wife helped me come to the reality that I am the expert of me, regardless of what any other persons says or thinks, and that mind-set was what allowed me to perform in a pressure-packed situation at the highest level possible. When we come to accept that we are the experts of ourselves, our minds accept that fact that our best is good enough and that we are capable no matter what challenges we face. We then trust ourselves to the point where we relinquish control of the outcome to happen as a natural cause and effect of our preparation and developed skill and talent. We allow ourselves to become an expression of our core, which is our true successful self.

9

TURN ON THE LIGHT

The sun was shining on this beautiful, clear, late, bay area fall day. As I walked out of the dark and dingy tunnel onto the bright green grass, my eyes took a bit to adjust, as the difference in light was so great. As I stepped foot on the green, moist grass of Candlestick Park, all of my memories of watching the likes of Jerry Rice, Joe Montana, Steve Young, Roger Craig, and many other great ones came streaming through my mind. Here I was getting ready to face the Forty-Niners in Candlestick on a field that had such a rich tradition of great, legendary football.

As I made my way to midfield to begin our pregame warm-ups, I was immersed in what I had to do to get my body ready to roll. Today was going to be a physical style of game because the Forty-Niners had a running game that was a smash-mouth running attack led by their workhorse, Frank Gore. As I was focused in our linebacker warm-up routine, I gathered that someone from the Forty-Niners side of the field was yelling at somebody on our side of the field. My gaze went toward the source of this loud, roaring voice.

The source of the lion's roar of a voice was a giant of a man. He had arms the size of tree trunks and a stature that was comparable to a big, burly bear. He was yelling not at someone specific but at our whole team. He was using his regular pre-game scare tactics to attempt to intimidate us by talking smack about how he and his team were going to eat us up and spit us out. He sounded like a hungry bear wanting to get something to eat, and we were who he wanted to feast on. Before his days as a Forty-Niner, he had been a staple for many years on the Dallas Cowboy offensive line. He helped plow open holes for hall-of-fame runner Emmitt Smith. He was an integral part in the '90s of the Dallas Cowboy Super Bowl teams. I remember him from watching him in my teenage years. What always stuck out about him, and I mean literally stuck out, was his backside.

I remember watching Jon Madden analyze Dallas Cowboy running plays. Whenever there was a shot from the backside of the Dallas offensive line, Jon Madden would pause the tape and make note of how big of a backside this guy had. He would draw a big circle around it to show how much junk he had in his trunk. I would describe his backside as a big bulldozer. It was about that wide, and he was about that powerful of a being. To say he was an intimidating opponent would be an understatement. His name was Larry Allen.

For the first time in a long time, an opponent's scare tactics actually worked. When we went into the locker room after warming up, I began to wonder if my life was on the line. All I could think about was during that week's film sessions in preparation leading up to the game, I saw big Larry Allen take a 350-pound defensive tackle of the Detroit Lions, pick him up by his throat, and toss him to the ground like a rag doll. It was impressive. No wonder he was as good as he was for so long. He was a powerful, strong, and mean dude. If Larry Allen had no problem tossing to the ground a 350 pounder, I wondered what he would do to me if he got a hold of me only weighing a mere 250 pounds. I started having second thoughts about confronting him.

I felt fear. I feared that he might get a hold of me and just crush me. I was trying to think of some survival techniques to avoid his powerful grasp. I couldn't really think of anything because that play of Larry Allen grabbing the 350-pound defensive tackle kept rerunning through my mind.

Going out onto the field for the first series, his smack talking continued. I swallowed a big gulp and figured I would test his bark versus his bite. I figured it would be the best way to see if he was all he had been hyped up to be. A few plays in the first series, there was a play where he had to come and block me. As I was reacting to my keys, I heard this growling like some animal was coming after me in the wild to take me as his prey. I saw that the big Larry Allen was coming after me to block me. As he was coming to block me, he was growling, and he put his massive arms out like he was going to try to envelop me. As he was coming toward me, in a split second I realized he looked like a player who was a bit too aggressive. I then reacted to defeat his attempt to pulverize me by giving him a little head fake and jab step. *Whiff!* He completely missed me, and didn't even touch me. Sure enough, I got in on the tackle. I jumped to my feet and thought, *Wait a minute! As long as I counter his power and strength with my quickness and speed, I'll be just fine.* In that moment I realized the fear I experienced was an illusion and complete fabrication of my own mind. Big Larry Allen was just another big guy who wasn't an indomitable animal but simply a human.

As the game continued, it was verified that the big Larry Allen was an overaggressive type, which caused him to sometimes get out of position on his blocks. I figured I would use his overaggressiveness against him. Late in the game on a crucial drive, it was third down and long. If we got off the field on this down, our offense then could run the clock out and we would basically win the game with the one stop.

We had a package in our defense where we would put three defensive linemen in the game, three linebackers, and five defensive backs. My role as one of the linebackers was to be either the fourth rusher if we chose to rush four or fake like I was going to rush and then drop into coverage and only rush three. It was a very deceptive blitz package. For this crucial third down and long situation we decided to use this three-three-five blitz package.

As the quarterback was going through his cadence, I was standing right over the big, burly Larry Allen. I told him I was going to run right over him and that as soon as that ball was snapped, he was going to get blasted. I could see him breathing harder and panting, getting himself ready to face my rush. At the snap of the ball, I gave him a quick jab step and faked like I going to rush, and then I bailed out and dropped into coverage. He flinched and fully expected me to take him on. I froze him just enough to free up our nose guard. It looked like Larry Allen was supposed to lend a little hand support to the center and help him if the nose guard took a route toward him. He was too caught up in trying to take me on as a rusher that he was late reacting to help the center. It resulted in a sack for our nose guard, and it put them in a fourth and long situation. We then were able to seal the victory.

I learned that the big Larry Allen was a big, aggressive football player, but he too was only human. As I overcame my fears of him somehow grasping hold of my neck and tossing me to the ground, I remained focused on playing my game and doing my job and ended up playing a fine game. The greatest opponent that day wasn't the daunting giant of a man who looked like a big, burly bear, but it was an opponent far more challenging and difficult to overcome—myself.

There are many daunting and great opponents we face in competitive situations. It can be our most bitter rival or the uncommon opponent we know little about. It could be an unknown opponent we have never seen but we know exists because we know that no matter how good we become, there is always someone out there who could be better than us at any given time. The greatest opponent, though, is the one we see on a daily basis.

It is the opponent we know the most about. We know what this opponent's likes and dislikes are. We know to the detail the greatest weaknesses and strengths of this opponent. We understand what can lead to its demise, and we understand what makes it tick. It is our most familiar opponent, and it is the most challenging opponent of them all. It is ourselves.

It's amazing what we can do if we just get out of our own way. Most of the time the way we really hinder ourselves is through our own fears. Most fears are imaginations of the mind, just like little children who fear monsters coming out from the closet or from under the bed when it is dark. The same can be said about those fears that come up when we are in pursuit of our true potential through competition. We begin to fear injury, failure, losing our abilities too soon, and what others or going to think or say about us. We fear sometimes being successful. We almost think we are not worthy to enjoy the gratification and joy that come from success.

When we face our fears head-on and confront them by not allowing them to debilitate us, we become more empowered and begin to build true confidence that is reflective of our true nature. By confronting our fears, we expose them and shed light in dark places, just like a child who turns on the light to see if there are truly monsters under the bed or in the closet, only to ultimately find that there are none to be found. On the contrary, if we shy away from our illusionary fears and allow them to affect our performance, we slowly weaken our heightened sense of resolve as we are taken hostage by an unreal force enticing us to shy away from achieving the highest standard of excellence.

10

COMPETITION, THE FUEL OF A CHAMPIONSHIP TEAM

When the news hit the wire, my heart sank, as it now seemed inevitable that this year (2008) was going to be my last season as a Green Bay Packer. My contract was going to be expiring this next season, and the Packers' front office had just signed an experienced, starting-caliber linebacker by the name of Brandon Chillar. He was slated to play in my same spot. He surely seemed like my replacement based on the size of the contract they had just signed him to. All of a sudden, my phone rang. On the other end was my linebackers' coach, Winston Moss. He asked if I had seen the news.

I said, "I did." He confirmed that Brandon was being brought in to compete for my job. I responded by saying, "I am willing to accept that competition."

Coach Moss interjected by saying, "With the kind of money they just gave him, they may say it's a competition when in fact they may already have him pegged in as the starter." I hated those types of pretend competitions.

Winston then proceeded to tell me in an almost big-brother kind of fashion, "I don't know if you know, but they also want to sign you to a contract extension."

"What!" I blurted. "This just isn't making any sense."

Coach Moss concurred and then warned me about not feeling pressured to take a bad deal just because all of a sudden the Packers now had a little leverage on their side. I thanked him for the advice.

About five minutes later, I received a call from the number of the Lambeau Field offices. A call from this number only really meant one of two things—it was either something really good or something as equally as terrible, meaning you might be packing your bags and heading on out. I was thinking it was for a good reason, especially after I had just gotten off of the phone with Winston. But I thought, *In this business anything can happen.*

Expecting the worst, I answered the phone. On the other end of the phone was the assistant to the general manager at the time, Jon Schneider, who now is the general manager of the Super Bowl 48 champs the Seattle Seahawks. He asked, "Did you see the news about us signing Brandon?"

I said, "Yes sir."

He said, "How about you come down to a cafe by the facility? I want to sit down with you and talk about what that news means to you over some lunch."

I asked, "What is this about?"

He said, "We will talk about it when you get here, but it's all good." I hung up the phone and headed to meet with Jon over some lunch to hear what he had to say.

As I entered into the cafe, I spotted John. We ordered lunch and sat down at a table in the farthest, most remote corner of the restaurant. As we sat down, John scanned the room for members of the media and for any potential eavesdroppers. As he started to explain what was happening, he asked me one last time, "Am I talking too loud?" He wanted to ensure that no one else could hear our conversation. I thought, *Man, this is like some type of CIA secret ops kind of stuff. This should be interesting.*

He began by saying that the news in no way meant that I was on my way out. He made it clear that the philosophy of the team was to have competition in every position group. They believed that by bringing in Brandon, there would be a heightened level of competition not only at my spot, but there would be more competition for the whole linebacking core. Additionally they wanted more flexibility to put out on the field more-deceptive and less-predictable schemes. By adding a versatile linebacker like Brandon, they felt they could do that. He closed out by saying, "We would also like to reward you with a new deal." I now felt excited about the prospect of playing alongside Brandon and for things to come.

Brandon and I did compete head to head in training camp in 2008. This is what came of our head-to-head competition from the eyes of our linebackers' coach, Winston Moss. "Brady's had his best camp and his best preseason to date," linebackers coach Winston Moss said after Tuesday's practice. "He's played really well (and) done some very good things. He's as physical as ever, so it's been all positive with Brady. I've always said that Brady was going to take it not necessarily as a challenge between Brandon and himself but as a challenge to be the best he can be [with the signing of Brandon in the offseason]." Moss said, "He's taken that approach, and he's maxing out. He's doing things—nobody can ever be perfect every single day—where you're close to saying that's as good as Brady can play. I don't think there's a SAM linebacker in the business that's as physical at the point of attack as he is," Moss said. "Bar none, in the National Football League, if he's not the best, he's as good as anybody."

Brady, along with teammates Brandon Chillar (54), and Nick Collins (36) taking on the Chicago Bears during the 2008 season.

The design of bringing Brandon in to add another element of competition worked with me. I was playing at a level I had never touched before. That was because Brandon's presence was pushing me there. I appreciated him for that. The 2008 year ended up being one of my best years of football.

I gained a better understanding of the idea that the more good players you have, the better the internal competition of the team, the better the team will perform overall. Unexpectedly, I saw another player who would be perfect to add that type of element of competition to our team. His name is Clay Matthews III. I first saw Clay play ball while watching a college football game with my longtime friend and roommate, AJ Hawk.

THE TRUE SPIRIT OF COMPETITION

From left to right. Clay Matthews (52), Brady Poppinga (51) and AJ Hawk (50) preparing to take on the Arizona Cardinals in the wildcard game in the 2009 NFL playoffs.

As was our custom when we played on the road, Saturdays were spent in a nice hotel resting and relaxing in preparation for the next day's game. Most guys like to go to the nearest mall or shopping center and relax by shopping and hanging out. My roomie, AJ, and I preferred to stay in our rooms and hang out, watching college football games. On this particular dark and cold fall day in Detroit, Michigan, we perused through the sports channels, looking for a good college football game. We ended up settling on watching AJ's alma matter, the Ohio State Buckeyes, play the USC Trojans. And boy was USC dominating this game. One player just kept catching my eye because of the big plays he was making and his style. He played a fanatical and tough style of football. As he played, his long, blond hair would whip around all over the place as it stuck out the back of his helmet. With almost comic book–looking biceps, he looked like the real life version of Thor. He played very similarly to AJ, me, and the other linebackers on our team. It was like I had found another kindred spirit, so much so that I mentioned to AJ, "We need to draft this guy." AJ said something to effect that that would be cool. But I wasn't joking. After watching him play, I prayed that we would bring him in. I wanted him on our team. He looked like the kind of guy who could really help us establish the right mind-set and help us contend for and win championships.

Unfortunately for the team, 2008 didn't work out too well for us. We finished the season with a six and ten mark. Changes came in the off season. Our defensive philosophy changed from a four down lineman, three linebacker base set, to a three down lineman, four linebacker set. The nature of my position changed as now I was transitioned to more of a rushing linebacker role like a defensive end instead of playing the traditional off-the-ball linebacker like I had come to master my first four seasons in the NFL.

In this offseason, everyone on the team was put on notice. We all knew from the GM on down that having another repeat six and ten season would mean that wholesale changes would come, meaning a lot of people would lose their jobs. The competition meter jumped a few notches. In this year's draft, the first pick we chose was a nose guard out of Boston College by the name of BJ Raji, who added competition to the defensive line. The second pick in the first round we chose Clay Matthews III, just as I had hoped. Many people called me and asked if the team picking Clay bothered me, since he and I both played the same position. I said,

THE TRUE SPIRIT OF COMPETITION

"Nope. I am actually really excited about that choice. He will be a great addition to help our team win."

With time Clay eventually proved to be one of the best defensive players in the game. It was clear that this year there was no messing around. The coaches were going to have a full cupboard of goods to work with. We as players had our work cut out for us because everywhere we looked, someone was hungry to not only take playing time away from you but also to take your job.

Training camp was intense. Everyone was on edge, from the GM on down. Since we were implementing a new defense, for the first few days everyone on defense was playing a step slow and not as intensely as we should since we were thinking more about trying to learn our new positions and responsibilities than just letting loose and playing. In one of our outside linebacker meetings, our coach, Kevin Greene, one of the all-time best outside linebackers ever to play, was perceptive of the lack of intensity we were playing with as a defense. He extended to us a challenge. He said in his intense voice that sounded like a WWE wrestler, "I need one of you guys, when you get a chance, to just blow up an offensive player. I will take the heat for it. Let's see who will do that."

When you practice against your own team, like we were doing in training camp, there was always a focus on playing hard against one another but being aware of keeping each other healthy. In most cases, in the NFL, injuries to a team can be the quickest way to go from being a contender to having a hard time just winning a game, so protecting your teammates, especially if they are in a vulnerable spot, was a priority. What Kevin was challenging us to do was to send a message to the whole team that our play needed to improve or success would be really hard to find that year. It wasn't a call to hurt anybody but a way to raise everyone's game. We all were aware of the risks associated with taking a shot like that. But when you give linebackers a challenge to go and do what we not only love to do but are born, trained, and destined to do, which is to deliver bone-crushing blows within the rules of the game of football, that challenge was music to our ears. Since our outside linebacker group was made up of some of the most competitive humans in the world, there was no doubt that there would be a race to see who would be the one to deliver the big, bone-crushing hit to wake us up.

As practice went on that day, we were all trying to find the right opportunity to get that one big-time shot that would just ignite the attitude of the whole defense. Late in practice, during a team drill, my chance came. It was a play on a rare occasion where I was dropping into coverage. Usually I was a rusher. As I picked up the quarterback and the direction to where he was going to throw the ball, I looked at both the quarterback and the running back, who looked like he would be the one to receive the pass, at the same time with my peripheral vision to get as fast of a jump on the throw as possible. As soon as the QB started with his throwing motion, I accelerated to where the running back was standing waiting for the pass to arrive. I wanted to hit him as hard as I possibly could to not only jar the ball loose but to also meet head-on the challenge Kevin Greene gave to us before practice. My sole focus was on the running back's midsection.

When I felt it was time, I launched my body, leading with my shoulder, putting all of the force of my 250-pound body with a ten-yard running start squarely in the midsection of the running back. As I engaged him, it felt like I ran through tissue paper because when you hit somebody just right, it's like hitting a baseball or a golf ball with the sweet spot of the bat or club. You don't even feel it. This was the case for me. As I ran through the running back, he flipped head over heels, landing directly on the back of his shoulders. The ball dislodged, and all mayhem broke loose.

After gathering myself after delivering such an aggressive blow, I was confronted not by one or two, but all the offensive linemen

THE TRUE SPIRIT OF COMPETITION

on the team. They were protecting their guy. I respected that. All I could do to defend myself was to grab my own facemask so my helmet wouldn't get ripped off and then cover up the family jewels and take whatever blows were being delivered as I was being swarmed by all the offensive linemen on the roster. Luckily I was wearing pads so I didn't feel one blow. In about two seconds, the cavalry arrived. My defensive teammates came to my side.

In the middle of this huge scrum, coaches intervened, breaking things up. As I jogged back to where the defense usually stands during practice, I heard the roar of the crowd in attendance. For a Packer training camp practice, it is pretty normal to average anywhere from ten thousand to twenty thousand fans per practice. The crowd started chanting, "Po-pping-a, Po-pping-a, Po-pping-a," over and over. As I made my way to the other side of the field, the mayhem continued. Coaches had to be restrained from one another. It was complete chaos.

Head coach Mike McCarthy found me and asked what happened. I explained to him that I had just made a clean, hard hit on the running back, attempting to dislodge the ball, which was exactly what I did, but with a little extra mustard. After the head coach, the general manger, Ted Thompson, came up to me. Like he would tell me every training camp because I always played full speed in practice with an intense, aggressive demeanor, he said, "Brady, you guys are on the same team. You have to protect each other."

I replied with a, "Yes sir."

At that point I was looking for Kevin Greene to see if he was going to hold to his word to where he would explain to the coaches and GM that he had challenged us outside linebackers to do just what I did—deliver a bone-jarring hit to get everyone going. I found Kevin in the crowd of players and coaches trying to get the head coach and GM's attention. He finally did and said, "That one was on me."

After everyone cooled their jets, we resumed practice. I will tell you what—Kevin was right. From that day forward, our defense played with a different energy. That year in 2009 as a defense, we broke the all-time Packer record for rushing defense, allowing the least amount of yards ever. I am not saying my huge hit in training camp was the only thing that factored into us playing strong defense in 2009. It was one of many factors. But the greatest factor behind us playing so well in 2009 was internal competition.

Even though we vastly improved in 2009 from 2008 by making the playoffs and narrowly losing in overtime to the eventual NFC champions the Arizona Cardinals in a shootout in the Wildcard Round, we as a team still felt we could improve. The only way to do that would be to again raise the competition meter the next season.

Competition for playing time this year, 2010, was like never before. On our two-deep depth chart on defense, we had at least twenty starting-caliber guys. That means that almost all the back-ups on the depth chart on defense could practically be a starter on other NFL teams. In training camp this time around, we didn't need any big, bone-crushing hits to get us going. We all had enough fire lit up under us with our respective position battles for playing time to keep us motivated and hungry.

When the regular season began, even if you weren't a starter, almost everyone played a lot. Internal competition on our team was so high that not only were we focused on defeating the guy on the opposing team, but we also had in the back of our minds that we had better make some huge plays so our playing time wouldn't diminish. That dynamic brought the best out of us all.

It was Monday night. I was enjoying the company of my family and recovering from the previous week's game, which was a big victory over a divisional opponent. My phone rang, and that dreaded number of the front office appeared on the caller ID. It was actually the perfect time during the season to trade me, cut me, or whatever. I answered the phone, again expecting to hear the worst. On the other end of the call was my outside linebackers coach, Kevin Greene. He said, "Brady, because of all the injuries to our inside linebackers, we are going to need to you to play inside linebacker this week."

I said, "Okay, no problem."

I was a bit annoyed since I was in the middle of trying to lock down the starting outside linebacker spot opposite to Clay Matthews. I was just starting to separate myself from the other guys. All week leading up to the next game, in which we were going to head to Washington and take on the Redskins, I practiced as an inside linebacker. My role was to just add depth. If all things went according to plan—meaning as long as everyone stayed healthy—I most likely wasn't going to see much action in this game.

After learning how to separate the way I operated from the swirling, uncontrollable forces around me, like playing time or what position I would be asked to play, all week long I prepared with my same attention to detail as I always attempted to and set my mind to be ready to roll at any time. On this particular Sunday in Washington, DC, it was a scorcher of a day. The temperature was up in the nineties, making it a day where in order to avoid muscle pulls and cramps, you had to stay well hydrated. The game was one of these back-and-forth defensive struggles. Neither team could take complete control of the game. During the game, on the sidelines I kept my mind in the game and stayed physically engaged by jumping on the stationary bicycle every twenty to thirty minutes and doing sprints to keep my body fired up.

Late in the third quarter, Clay Matthews came up lame. He had pulled a hammy and couldn't return to the game. Washington's offense began to use an up-tempo style, trying to take advantage of the absence of the pass rushing threat of Clay, since he was out with an injury. The outside linebackers in the game were gassed, and their level of production was minimal. I was essentially standing in Kevin Greene's hip pocket, and he turned to me and said, "Go in there for one of the other guys."

Not having practiced at that position all week, I lined up and felt comfortable and confident. In my mind I knew very well if I made some big plays in this game, I would earn an opportunity for more playing time in future games. I was not only competing against the Redskins on this day, but just like all the games before, I was also competing against my fellow outside linebackers for playing time. On my first play, it was a pass play. We called a defense to where we were only going to rush three. In this scenario, I knew very well I would have to deal with two blockers.

At the snap of the ball, I took two hard and fast steps upfield. I felt the guard and the tackle both turning toward me to block me. In an instant, I planted my upfield foot in the ground and shot the gap between both of the lineman. That move defeated both of the blockers. I now had a clear path toward the quarterback—Donovan McNabb. He was a big, agile quarterback who was tough to sack. When playing against a quarterback like him, it's one challenge to beat the block of the offensive line to get to the quarterback, and then a whole other challenge presents itself, which is trying to catch and tackle a quarterback like Donovan to the ground.

As I accelerated toward Donovan, he stepped up in the pocket to throw the ball. Since my angle was pointed to where he was at, not to where he ended up, I had to reach with my inside hand as I flew past him upfield to attempt to grab the back of his jersey and tear him to the ground. He was too big. Fortunately, though, I disrupted him enough to force an errant throw. That play set the tone for me in this game. I was going to end up playing arguably the best stretch of football of my career.

Following this play to finish out the fourth quarter I made five tackles, I had a QB hurry, and I was playing well both against the pass as a rusher and against the run. At the end of the fourth quarter, the score was locked up at thirteen all. You know what that means? Sudden death Overtime, meaning whoever scores first, whether it's a field goal or a touchdown, wins the game. In this scenario whoever wins the coin toss has the best chance to win the game. The Redskins won the coin toss. We were up first on defense and had to make a big stop to get the ball back to our offense. Kevin Greene saw that I had the hot hand and was outplaying the other outside linebackers, so he stayed with me the rest of the way.

After the first two plays of Washington's first series of overtime, we held them to third and long. Dom Capers, the "godfather" of the zone blitz, dialed one of his creative blitzes for this critical third-down play. He used a special package of players called a "psycho package." In this package, we would have on the field one defensive lineman, four linebackers, and six defensive backs. As linebackers we wouldn't line up and stay in the same place like most other downs. In this package we would be moving all over the place, looking to confuse the offense. I was moving from one side of the line to the other, and then at the last second I would be somewhere else. I did this to keep the offensive line guessing as to what angle I was going to rush from. No matter where I ended up with my alignment, the most important part was that at the snap of the ball, I would need to blitz with a track directly at the right guard.

The ball was snapped, and I accelerated right at the guard. Just as he shot his hands to push me off course and to stop my momentum, I knocked his hands down. With my speed and quickness, I turned the corner and accelerated toward the blindside of Donavan McNabb. I hit him as hard as possible attempting to dislodge the ball as I sacked him. Unfortunately for us, Donavan, with his big hands, held onto the ball. But with that critical sack, we stopped them and gave our offense the ball back, poised to win the game.

Even though Aaron that year had a stretch where he played at an all-time best level, on this drive he made a mistake. Deep in our own territory, he threw into triple coverage. Washington picked off the pass. To win the game, all Washington had to do was down the football a few times and then kick a chip shot field goal. That is exactly what they did to win the game.

Even though we had lost, I played the best stretch of football of my life. In only one quarter of play, I accumulated one sack, one QB hurry, one QB hit, one tackle for loss, and six tackles. That was a byproduct of the internal competition of our team. In order to see the field, you not only had to play well against the other team, but you also had to outperform the other players in your position group. On this day I was able to do that, getting the starting nod for the next game. The dynamics of this hypercompetitive environment elevated everyone's play to levels never before reached. Again we played stellar defense that year.

It was a good thing that we were so deep with talent as a team. Myself included, we had sixteen guys who ended up on the season-ending injured reserve list this year. Even so, that year we were still able to get hot at the right time, make a run, and win the Super Bowl. The winning of the Super Bowl was the fruit of a team built on competition.

When you look at the reasons why we won the Super Bowl, competition was the underlying theme. First, Aaron Rodgers's play during the last month of that season through the playoffs and Super Bowl was historic. You would be hard pressed to find a quarterback play as well as he did down the stretch like that in the history of football. It was impressive.

Aaron had the honor and privilege of backing up the legendary Brett Favre for three years of his career. When Aaron was drafted in the first round in the 2005 draft, Brett made it known that it wasn't in his contract to mentor the guy who would end up replacing him.

THE TRUE SPIRIT OF COMPETITION

Brett wasn't going to allow Aaron to feel comfortable upon his arrival to Green Bay.

Before a training camp practice in 2005 during mine and Aaron's first year with the Packers, there was a helmet that was being passed around the locker room by Brett for us all to sign. As Brett made his way to my locker, I initially thought it was another memorabilia signing request that we were fulfilling, as was a daily custom. The Packer fans are some of the most passionate fans there are in all of sports. They loved having you autograph just about anything. (Even their baby's forehead if they didn't have anything else for you to sign. I actually had that request.) So I didn't think much about autographing the helmet until Brett handed it over to me with a mischievous smirk. As I grabbed the helmet, I noticed that it wasn't a replica helmet like most are that we autograph. It was the helmet of one of our teammates. Being a rookie, I wasn't about to question Brett on the origin of the helmet he was having the team autograph. But I sensed something was suspicious. I signed my John Hancock on the side of the helmet, finished readying myself, and went off to start practice.

At the beginning of practice, we would start off doing individual drills where each position would go to their assigned spot on the field and work their techniques and fundamentals. The quarterback's individual fundamental drills were always grabbing our attention since Favre always kept things exciting. As I was taking my rest during my individual drills, I heard a big uproar over in the QB drills section of the field. I saw Favre laughing so hard that he looked like he was going to fall over. Who was he laughing at? As I took a closer look at who he was mocking, I gathered that it was Aaron Rodgers, who happened to be wearing a helmet with all of our team members' signatures on it. I thought, *So that's whose helmet we all were signing.*

From the day Aaron arrived in 2005 to the day Favre left

the Packers in 2008, those two always competed. Even though there was never an open quarterback competition between the two, they competed against one another day in and day out. They were always looking to outdo each other. The main thing they would compete in was in the individual drills for the quarterbacks. The equipment guys would set up these nets that faced toward the sky that were about three feet in diameter, placed fifty yards or so from where the quarterbacks were doing their drills. The quarterbacks then would have a contest to see who could throw the most balls into these nets before individual drills would end.

Whenever you saw a quarterback throw a ball into one of these nets, all who were watching would cheer in pure amazement because to be able to do that requires a world-class arm that maybe at one time only three people in the world would have. Green Bay was fortunate to have two of those three world-class arms at one time. Favre and Aaron would go back and forth throwing the football into the nets. Whenever a ball left their hands, it was like it was shot out of a cannon. It was unbelievable to witness. Although Favre was extremely accurate, to my recollection Aaron won most of those battles. That didn't sit too well with Favre.

Many people forget that when Aaron first showed up in Green Bay, he was challenged to retool his throwing motion. By the time Aaron became a full-time starter, do you know whose throwing motion he had adopted? It looked very close to Brett Favre's. Competing with and watching Brett as his backup showed Aaron what it took to be an elite QB. Also, when Aaron was just beginning his first season as the starter in 2008, the Packers drafted in the second round Brian Brohm. Most second rounders are drafted to be given a long, hard look as a starter. Aaron again rose to the challenge of having a second rounder come in and compete for playing time. Aaron dominated that challenge so much

THE TRUE SPIRIT OF COMPETITION

that today it is not even talked about as a challenge. Competition drove Aaron to play at an historic level in 2010, when it counted the most.

Brady celebrating the Super Bowl XLV championship with his wife Brooke.

The second reason why we won the Super Bowl was because of the edge and toughness the overall team displayed. After having to deal with impactful player after player getting hurt, the team didn't flinch. That was due to the culture of competition that team was built on. That culture created a collective mind-set to where facing and overcoming adversity was an everyday occurrence. When the team had to deal with so many good players getting injured, the team did what they were conditioned and trained to do, and that was to simply keep competing independent of any outside uncontrollable forces, like injuries.

Competition was the fuel that led to our Super Bowl Championship in 2010. The culture of competition brought the best out of all of us, especially in some of the most pressure-packed situations. When you embrace the true spirit of competition by welcoming the challenges presented to you by moments of opposition, your resolve and determination in adverse situations sharpen. As all of us members of the 2010 Green Bay Packers Super Bowl team witnessed, competition then works like a springboard, catapulting you to higher levels of performance and achievement.

11

CONCLUSION: AMATEUR SPORTS—THE BUSINESS OF DEVELOPING THE CHARACTER OF THE YOUTH THROUGH COMPETITION

One by one the lights surrounding the baseball diamond began to go dark except for one, leaving just enough light to be able to gather your equipment and make your way out of the ballpark. Disappointed because we had just lost and been eliminated from the baseball tournament, I gathered my personal baseball equipment and packed my baseball bag. I put one of my arms through one of the straps of the bag, swung it on my back, put my other arm through the other strap, and carried the bag like a backpack. As I left the dugout to find my parents to walk to our car together, to my surprise, I heard two grown men yelling at one another with an angry tone. Immediately this tense, awkward feeling flooded the ambiance as their rage directed at one another increased. The two men yelling were a parent of one of my teammates and one of the coaches. The coach was still on the field while the parent was throwing his verbal jabs from the stands.

I felt scared that those two grown men, who I looked up to, were going to get into a physical confrontation. If it wasn't for the twenty or so feet between the two, the next step in the escalation of their disagreement would have been to get physical. They yelled at each other without regard for us kids or for the parents standing around us. They were swearing at each other and saying things that would be inappropriate to say even around kids in their teens. They were losing control of the situation and themselves.

The frustration of both of these men stemmed from the fact that we had just lost to a team that on paper, should have never beaten us. This confrontation was only making matters worse. The parent felt that if his son would have played more, we would have won, which I agreed with, although he was going about this all wrong. Instead the coach chose to play his son. The parent felt his son was a better player and should have never sat on the bench while the coach's son played. The irony is, when the parent volunteered to coach, he favored his son in the same way.

It would have been nice to have memories of some of my big hits, the friends I made, or what I learned, not only about baseball but about life. But instead, what is etched in my mind as the most vivid memory of this year of baseball is two grown men contentiously arguing over what could have been done differently to win a game. Their obsession with winning deceived them into thinking the game was about them more than the kids who were playing. That was a serious mistake and oversight on their part.

These types of conflicts happen all the time in sports, from little league on up to the highest levels of competition. The root problem lies with an over-obsession with winning. The passion to win and the over-obsession with winning are sometimes mistaken for one another. Being passionate about winning and having that passion be the fuel to your competitive fire is healthy. This is what the thrill of competition is about. But the over-obsession with winning is a whole different matter. The difference between the two is subtle but noticeable. The passion to win is an intense emotional energy that we control. It propels us to high levels of success. It is the main driving force that motivates us to ambitiously pursue victory. The obsession to win is a restrictive emotional energy that controls us. It drives us to do very hurtful and selfish acts in the name of winning.

One of the ways we as a society use to justify crossing the line into the realm of being over-obsessed with winning is when we try to emulate the pros at the amateur level. Many think that since the professional levels are the highest levels of competition in the world, that at the amateur level, we need to operate like the professionals to be truly successful. From the outside looking in, the passion and drive to win at the professional level sometimes comes across as obsessive when most of the time, it isn't. It is understandable to see where that misinterpretation can happen.

The nature of the professional level is that you are in the business of winning championships. Because of that, there is an extreme, intense urgency to win, which there should be. That is because at the professional level, everyone accepts the rules of engagement. You know that in the three big sports in the United States, football, basketball, and baseball, as a player, coach, or executive, big bucks are invested in you to put your respective teams in position to win championships. If you don't, it is understood that you may be fired from your job, and hence there is a higher level of urgency placed on winning. Even though it is not their initial intent, in a world where the line between being over-obsessed with winning and placing a high level of urgency on winning is razor thin, there will be times when they cross over to the extreme of being over-obsessed with winning. But even at that level, crossing into the world of being overly obsessed with winning is unhealthy and can be damaging.

At a little league or amateur level, you couldn't be further from the pressure of having to win like the professionals. The professional level is the business of winning. In contrast, the amateur level is the business of developing the character of the youth through competition. At the little league level the number-one priority should be first and foremost having fun. Many say, "The only way to have fun is to win." That thinking is unequivocally wrong because if it's the only way to have fun, then what happens if a team plays their best and still loses? Or even worse, what happens to that unfortunate team who over the span of a little league season continually improves but doesn't win a game at all? (I have personally been in that situation a few times.)

Clearly, there is absolutely nothing wrong with being passionate about winning. Even though losing is never fun, the reality is that at any level of competition, winning every game is very unlikely and isn't guaranteed. The way to ensure that the little leaguers have the most fun, regardless of the outcome of the games, is accomplished by celebrating the small day-to-day victories that are in their control and that come from day-to-day improvements of their skill development. That way fun becomes a controllable result of the day-to-day victories of improvement that are a function of the process of winning games.

While turning the focus to the day-to-day improvements, the little leaguers will learn a process-based approach to competition. If you talk to any performance coach or champion, a process-based approached, which is placing your focus on the day-to-day activities that lead to victory, is most effective in accessing the highest levels

THE TRUE SPIRIT OF COMPETITION

of performance. On the other hand, the results-based approach that puts the focus squarely on just the outcome, whether you win or lose, actually leads to lower levels of performance.[1] To ensure that those who are participating in little league or amateur sports are having the most fun and enjoying themselves, it is essential that the pressure to win is redirected to the process of winning.

This approach is sound for two reasons. First, it actually creates the highest probability to win, and it makes having fun something that can be controlled, independent of the win/loss record. Second, it preserves a laid back and fun environment for the youth to thrive in.

Keeping the atmosphere loose and stress-free at the amateur level is so important because the majority of kids at that level just aren't as deeply invested in winning as the higher levels. They have other interests, like school, music, other sports or hobbies, and activities that take up a lot of their time and attention. Additionally, at all amateur levels, there will be participants participating for the first time in their lives in the sport of their choice.

By comparison, at the professional level, your job is your respective sport. You could spend anywhere from eighty hours on up per week exclusively working on your craft, through training, practice, or playing games. The majority of professionals are masters of their trade, meaning they have been perfecting their sport the majority of their lives. It is unfair to place the same amount of pressure on these kids at an amateur level to perform and win as you would with a professional. Those who compete at the amateur level are not conditioned to deal with that kind of pressure. If you do place more pressure on them to win than they can handle, the fun will go away. Once the fun is taken away, that is when the kids suffer and more harm than good is done.

---

1 Michael Lardon, Finding Your Zone. (New York: Penguin Group, 2008), 131–4.

At any level, whether you're in little league, or in the professional ranks, being overly obsessed with winning is not healthy and is destructive. Finding out if you are crossing into the line of being overly obsessed with winning is easy. Ask yourself the following questions:

1. Is it worth it to physically or emotionally harm one of your family members, friends, neighbors, or those around you if it means you will win?
2. Is it worth it to put performance-enhancing substances in your body to gain an edge to win, even if it means later in life you may risk having serious health issues?
3. Is winning the antidote to everything?
4. Does winning make me feel like I am above my opponent?
5. Does the thought of dealing with defeat to the hands of my opponent cause me to feel hostile toward my opponent?
6. Does congratulating my opponent following a great performance on his or her end feel like it takes something away from me?

If you answered yes to any one of these questions you are either walking the line or have crossed the line into the overly obsessed with winning territory. In the news quite often you will hear of people who cross that line and do the most heinous acts that turn out to be destructive and regrettable. The reality is, at some point, all of us have done something to one degree or another that we regretted after the fact that was induced by being over-obsessed with winning.

The key of bridling our passion for winning is to compete consciously. It is important in the heat of competition, as our passion for winning runs high, for us to stay aware of how competition affects us. While immersed in the heat of competition, if we are

THE TRUE SPIRIT OF COMPETITION

enjoying the journey of rising to the competitive moment; if we are having fun while passionately attempting to win; if we improve regardless of the outcome; if we feel competition is pulling our best selves out of us, then these are strong indicators we are on the right track. On the other hand, if we realize that the enjoyment of the pursuit of victory is unfulfilling and empty; if we feel excessive pressure to avoid defeat at all costs, enticing us to want to cheat or physically or emotionally tear others down to gain an advantage because we can't bear losing; or if it seems that being in the heat of competition causes us to lose control over our emotions, then we need to reevaluate why we are engaging in the pursuit of the thrill of victory. We are going to need to make changes so competition becomes more of a positive experience. If not, it is very easy to slip into that mode of being over-obsessed with winning, which more times than not results in a fleeting feeling of short-term satisfaction at the cost of long-term pain and regret.

In my youth when I competed from a place of fear of being labeled a failure, the error I made was in underestimating who I was as a person. My over-obsession with winning was triggered by a survival mechanism that would click on when I felt my successful self was in danger of dying. I wrapped my mind around the idea that losing was death—death to my successful self. I mistakenly felt that an outcome of a competition defined my self-worth.

What I eventually learned was that even being labeled as the best to ever play the game (and by the way, to be considered one of the best to ever play or do anything is one of the greatest accomplishments one could ever achieve) still falls short of the reality of how truly great we all are. There are no labels, titles, or descriptive words that fully encompass who we are at the core. Our core-selves are so great that they exist independently of any successes we can accomplish or attain. This means our successful self is always alive and will never die, regardless of the number of losses we have or failures we may face. The only time our successful self becomes inaccessible is if we deny ourselves of our true identity. That occurs within a competitive environment when we mistakenly believe our core or worth as a person hinges on the outcome of a competition.

The only way to make our core selves manifest is to make a conscious choice to be an expression of them. Epictetus of old described as good as anyone how you do that. He said, "Tentative efforts lead to tentative outcomes. Therefore, give yourself fully to your endeavors. Decide to construct your character through excellent actions, and determine to pay the price for a worthy goal. The trials you encounter will introduce you to your strengths. Remain steadfast … and one day you will build something that endures, something worthy of your potential." When we compete by making a conscious choice to fully commit all of our strength and energy to come out victorious, no matter what the outcome is, our successful selves will emerge.

With this perspective of competing from a higher ground, winning becomes a byproduct along the path of self-actualization, meaning that when we see competition as a way of fulfilling our potential, we tap into the vast reservoir of greatness that is within us all. Wins and losses become resources along the process. Losses become learning tools, and wins become valuable marks we hit along the path that indicate we are making progress in the right direction. The many different forms of the opponents we face become the vehicles that guide us along this path. As we face our fears with a competitive zeal, we come to realize they were illusions of the mind that, once confronted, immediately disappear. Instantaneously fear is replaced with faith and confidence that we are capable. At certain times along the way, we will stop and see how far we have come. We will appreciate the challenges and different forms of adversities we

THE TRUE SPIRIT OF COMPETITION

have faced along the way because we know that without them, our greatest accomplishments wouldn't have been possible.

The nature of our existence is that we all compete, no matter whether we are athletes or not. All people will face a situation where they will be challenged in some way, shape, or form. In the instance, when we choose to face that challenge head-on and look to overcome it, we will have engaged our competitive spirit. Our opponent may be the most unlikely of opponents, but as soon as we accept that challenge that the opponent places in front of us, instantly we will know that the ability to overcome such a challenge is within us already. That is when we will fully practice and understand the true spirit of competition.

CPSIA information can be obtained
at www.ICGtesting.com
Printed in the USA
FFOW03n1600141114
8752FF